SING
MARY'S SONG

AN ADVENT MESSAGE
OF HOPE AND DELIVERANCE

JOHN A. STROMAN

UPPER
ROOM BOOKS®
NASHVILLE

Cover image: The Annunciation, by Gustave Doré
Cover design: Left Coast Design, Portland, OR / www.lcoast.com
Interior implementation: PerfecType, Nashville, TN

Library of Congress Cataloging-in-Publication Data
Stroman, John A.
  Singing Mary's song : an Advent study of deliverance and hope / by John A. Stroman.
      p. cm.
  ISBN 978-0-8358-1118-7 — ISBN 978-0-8358-1120-0
  1. Advent--Prayers and devotions. 2. Mary, Blessed Virgin, Saint--Prayers and devotions. I. Title.
  BV40.S765 2012
  242'.332--dc23
                    2011053106

Printed in the United States of America

TABLE OF CONTENTS

INTRODUCTION

When Mary learns that she will give birth to the Messiah, she sings an aria of freedom. Her song presents no sweet lullaby in anticipation of her baby's birth but a message of freedom and hope for the homeless, the hungry, the refugee, the abused and misused, the powerless, and the despairing. These words express a vision for a better future: "[God] has brought down the powerful from their thrones, and lifted up the lowly" (Luke 1:52). Her song captures the words of hope from Hannah and Miriam and echoes the cry of deliverance from the Exodus, "Let my people go!" Mary passes these words of hope into the world, where Jesus proclaims this theme of deliverance in his inaugural sermon: "The Spirit of the Lord is upon me, because he has anointed me to bring good news to the poor . . . and to let the oppressed go free" (Luke 4:18).

Charles Wesley captured the same theme in the lyrics of his Advent hymn, "Come, thou long-expected Jesus, born to set thy people free." I find Advent one of the most uplifting and inspiring seasons of the Christian year because we hear again that we are not alone in our struggles: Immanuel—God is with us!

Mary's words of liberation and freedom set the stage for the beginning of a new sense of deliverance and hope for a dark and fearful world. The word hail means to greet with enthusiastic acclaim and welcome. This Advent let us say, "Hail, Mary!"

THE MARY OF THE BIBLE

The biblical account of Advent is rooted in Old Testament events, beginning when God promised Abram, "In you all the families of the earth shall be blessed" (Gen. 12:3). For Christians, the promise to Abram reached its fullest expression of deliverance in the birth of Jesus. In the biblical narrative from the Exodus to Bethlehem, we discover that God's main concern is deliverance (a theme expressed in the ninth-century hymn lyrics traditionally sung on the first Sunday of Advent, "O come, O come, Emmanuel, and ransom captive Israel" [UMH 211]). Mary's canticle lifts the curtain on a new chapter of God's activity, accomplishing what the apostle Paul calls "a new creation" (see Gal. 6:15). God has taken the initiative to reveal the Divine self to us in a manner never previously accomplished.

After an instant of fear and doubt following the angel's annunciation, Mary declared, "Here am I, the servant of the Lord; let it be with me according to your word" (Luke 1:38). From this moment on, all generations will call her "blessed." The world will never be the same.

In our study we will see how scripture presents Mary as one whose importance extends beyond the Annunciation and birth narrative into the life of the church. She is the only New Testament character present at Jesus' birth, at the Crucifixion, and at the Day of Pentecost. That is to say, Luke's Gospel portrays Mary not just as a mother but also as a disciple and a prophet. But in Luke's portrayal of her as a worrying, troubled mother, Mary becomes the most interesting part of his story. Even after the wondrous circumstances surrounding the birth of her son, there seem to have been times when she did not comprehend who he was and the full implications of his ministry.

Mary "pondered in her heart" what she had undergone as she tried to accept certain realities that went beyond her understanding (Luke 2:19). She believed when there was no evidence to do so. In pondering, Mary kept these matters in mind, holding them at the center of her being until the truth was disclosed. The scriptures record few of Mary's words, "but we can know that if Mary gave birth to Jesus and did the work of mothering, she likely experienced each of these sentiments and much, much more. She knew Jesus first, foremost, and most profoundly."[1] We will explore how Mary persevered as disciple, prophet, and mother with a certain kind of "Christian spiritual presence" of faith and prayer.

Beverly Gaventa points out that if Protestants are to talk about Mary, they must begin in a "Protestant-like" way. "That is to say we must begin with Scripture."[2] Within the scriptures Mary stands out as an important character, significant in her own right. She remains primarily the mother of Jesus, who followed him to his death and beyond. But the Magnificat suggests that she was an extraordinary reader of scripture as well, capable of weaving passages into a new song of deliverance and hope, a song that has become one of the most frequently sung hymns in church history.

But for most Protestants, Mary remains almost invisible. We see her at Advent and Christmas, but by Epiphany she disappears. Historically, Protestant thought has protested certain Catholic practices, including a protest against Mariology (the devotion of Mary that goes beyond scripture). Consequently, Protestants have lost sight of Mary's substantial role in the biblical narrative. "Mary was never part of my Presbyterian experience, but after all she was the mother of Jesus. Whether or not your personal faith includes *Theotokos,* the mother of God, she deserves recognition in the story of salvation and in our piety."[3]

In focusing on Mary's life, I have intentionally limited myself to the biblical text; by doing so, we can gain a fresh approach to scripture. The Mary in the New Testament is believable. She knew life as we know life. If that were not true, there would not have been an Incarnation, the Word becoming flesh. The Incarnation stands as Mary's greatest achievement, forming the heart of the biblical narrative of deliverance and hope. Through the birth of her child, God is with us. God entered the real world of flesh-and-blood human beings. Through Mary, God became incarnate, embodied, and fully present in our world. We affirm this fact every time we repeat the words of the creed, "born of the Virgin Mary."

PATTERN FOR THIS ADVENT STUDY

Daily readings and prayers are provided for the entire season of Advent. At the end of each day, reflection questions offer a means of gathering and processing what you have read and thought about that day.

You may use the book for individual devotions or in conjunction with a small-group study. The Leader's Guide for small-group sessions is found in the back of the book (page 97).

- *If you are using the book as an individual,* begin reading on the first Sunday of Advent.
- *If you are using the book for a small-group study,* begin reading on the Sunday prior to the first Sunday of Advent. Then you will be ready to discuss the readings and scripture at your first meeting. The pattern will continue as follows:

Read Week 1	Meet to discuss on First Sunday of Advent
Read Week 2	Meet to discuss on Second Sunday of Advent
Read Week 3	Meet to discuss on Third Sunday of Advent
Read Week 4	Meet to discuss on Fourth Sunday of Advent

The Leader's Guide outlines the four sessions. These incorporate group sharing and an exercise for deeper engagement with the biblical text in a framework of prayer and song.

- Week 1 focuses on Mary and the birth of Jesus; her relationships with Joseph, Elizabeth, and Zechariah; and her visit to the Temple and encounter with Simeon and Anna.
- Week 2 focuses on Galatians 4:4. Considering the many factors in the Greco-Roman world that converged at the time of Jesus' birth, we recognize that God indeed had an appointed time for the birth of Christ.
- Week 3 explores the meaning of Mary and Joseph's flight into Egypt.
- Week 4 guides us in preparing both our minds and hearts for Christmas Day.

ACKNOWLEDGMENTS

I am grateful for those who have shared their stories of faith and hope with me through my many years in the parish ministry. I have related a few of these stories, and for each story I have deep appreciation and respect, having obtained permission to use it. In some cases I have used pseudonyms and altered some details to preserve individuals' privacy.

WEEK 1: SINGING MARY'S SONG

MARY SINGS

*"[The Lord] has looked with favor on the lowliness of his servant.
Surely, from now on all generations will call me blessed."*

LUKE 1:48

THEME

God uses unlikely vessels to bring the message of hope and deliverance.

SUNDAY

God's Promises Fulfilled in Unexpected Ways

SCRIPTURE READING • LUKE 1:26-40

The birth narratives teach us to be attentive to what often seems obscure or inconspicuous, like a mustard seed, a bit of leaven—or a baby born in a manger. In a world of fast-paced media and spectacular special effects, being attentive becomes difficult. But often the most influential events occur in a rather secretive and almost imperceptible fashion.

The Advent of Christ provided no exception. The Messiah's coming was not unexpected (having been anticipated for centuries), but the circumstances of his coming proved a surprise. God chose to come into the world in a low-key, almost casual way, shunning the spectacular and preferring the ordinary. What could be more ordinary than the birth of a baby?

God had previously appeared in humble and ordinary ways—when Moses turned aside to see the burning bush (Exod. 3:3), and when God spoke to Elijah in a "still small voice" (1 Kings 19:12, KJV). The same was true when God came to earth as a child. Jesus (who was fully divine) often presented a humble presence. To many he looked merely like a child born in poverty and obscurity, a young man growing up unrecognized and unacknowledged in his hometown, a man entering a city on a donkey, a prisoner refusing to answer the false accusations of a judge, and a criminal dying on a cross. Jesus' coming proved to be so ordinary that the masses overlooked him.

The apostle Paul helps us to understand God's plan.

> God chose what is foolish in the world to shame the wise; God chose what is weak in the world to shame the strong; God chose what is low and despised in the world, things that are not, to reduce to nothing things that are, so that no one might boast in the presence of God (1 Cor. 1:27-29).

This Advent is no different. Christ continues to manifest himself in the same way. We may expect to see Christ disclosed in familiar carols and be surprised to recognize him in the cacophony of sounds at the shopping mall. We may expect him to come in the familiar language of the Bible only to hear his voice in some strange new tongue that we initially find foreign or even offensive. But we shouldn't be surprised when the Messiah reveals himself not just in our well-lit and decorated homes and churches but also in our streets, on our college campuses, and to the forgotten people in the dark corners of the earth.

This Advent let us focus on one person in particular who was surprised by God's presence—a seemingly inconspicuous and lowly person who became the instrument and vessel of God's hope and peace. This season we consider Mary, the mother of Jesus. Just as God appears in unlikely circumstances, so God tends to choose persons who do not fit the "job description," like Sarai, Moses, Hannah, Ruth, David, Esther, and now Mary. Yet these persons turn out to be instruments of great events.

The story of Jesus' birth fits into the unfolding of the biblical drama, which wound its way from God's promise to Abram (Gen. 12:3) through the dramatic story of slavery, bondage, exile, and liberation and reached its climactic fulfillment when the angel appeared to Mary.

The Advent story begins at the Annunciation, the announcement by the angel Gabriel to Mary that she would conceive and bear the Son of God. We can imagine it happening so quickly that Mary became spellbound! An angel appeared speaking the words, "Greetings, favored one! The Lord is with you." What could this possibly mean? Before Mary could catch her breath, the angel declared, "You will conceive in your womb and bear a son, and you will name him Jesus. He will be great, and will be called the Son of the Most High." At first, Mary may not have fathomed the magnitude of her role in this drama. The angel bade her, "Do not be afraid" (Luke 1:30), but she must have been afraid. As a teenager, unmarried and (soon to be) pregnant, living in a patriarchal society with little status and no power, she faced a future of shame or punishment. Luke gives no indication that she received any parental support. She was probably not just frightened. She was most likely terrified.

Overwhelmed, Mary considered what to do next. Remembering the words of the angel telling her that her cousin Elizabeth was six months pregnant, Mary went with haste to Elizabeth's house seeking a refuge in her time of need.

During Advent we may also want to seek out a place of refuge, a special place where we can escape from everything that overwhelms us. Just as the stars may be obscured by pollution and the glare of the city lights, so also the light, hope, love, joy, and peace of the Advent message can be obscured by the noise of shopping malls, the ever-present consumerism, the myriad parties and celebrations, and the persistent media buzz. We need to uncover that place this Advent where we can be silent, reflective, and prayerful. During this time of waiting, our eyes, ears, and minds can adjust to the radiant presence of God's love for us in Jesus Christ. May our hearts echo the expectations of the well-known Shaker hymn, "Simple Gifts":

'Tis the gift to be simple,
'Tis the gift to be free.
'Tis the gift to come down where we ought to be.

Mary underwent sudden and dramatic change and became perplexed and afraid. She asked the angel, "How can this be, since I am a virgin?" But then she heard and trusted the words of the angel and went to share her experience with her cousin Elizabeth. In spite of her fear and uncertainty, she was able to sing!

The opening words of her song of deliverance and hope proclaim,

> My soul magnifies the Lord,
>   and my spirit rejoices in God my Savior.
> —Luke 1:46-47

Mary's song of freedom sets the stage for Christians everywhere as we begin our journey through Advent.

Singing Mary's Song reminds us that God comes among us in the most unexpected ways.

1. Where did Jesus, God-With-Us, come to you today?
2. What challenges or barriers—emotional, spiritual, practical—prevented you from experiencing Advent today?
3. This Advent we have the opportunity to prepare for a special guest. How can you prepare your home, family, and heart for Immanuel, "God is with us"?
4. How can you shift your gaze from the bright lights and glitz of the holiday season to the small and inconspicuous? How can you be ready for what God wants to reveal to you?
5. How do you see Jesus' birth as a continuation of God's plan for salvation and freedom from bondage? From what has Jesus set you free? What bonds does he seek to break in your life?
6. What allowed Mary to discover faith and song in chaos and fear?

Prayer: O Lord, as we begin this journey that requires awareness and preparation, help us to seek a quiet place where we may hear the message you have for us. May we ponder with Mary the amazing ways in which you choose to speak to us. Amen.

MONDAY

God Continues to Seek Deliverance of God's People

SCRIPTURE READING • LUKE 1:41-55

Imagine the scene. Mary, all out of breath, arrives at Elizabeth's home. Elizabeth recognizes both fear and excitement in Mary's eyes as she reaches out to embrace her, declaring, "Blessed are you among women, and blessed is the fruit of your womb. And why has this happened to me, that the mother of my Lord comes to me?" (Luke 1:42-43). Then the miracle child in Elizabeth's womb does a "dance of joy."

Despite the doubt and fear that came before, Mary's encounter with Elizabeth was a joyful one. Both women, undergoing seemingly impossible pregnancies, have known the mysterious intervention of the Holy Spirit. We see a pregnant teenager embraced by an older woman, also pregnant, and who thought herself beyond childbearing years. When Mary heard Elizabeth's words of blessing and love, the magnitude of the moment must have dawned on her: *As poor, as frightened, and as young as I am, God has chosen me!*

Was Mary aware that her son would unleash a force of love in the world that would change it forever? Maybe this awareness filled her with gratitude so great that it overflowed into song.

As Mary began her song, we might picture her wrapped in the mantle of her ancestor, Miriam, who beat on the tambourine at the Red Sea and sang, "Sing to the LORD, for he has triumphed gloriously; horse and rider he has thrown into the sea" (see Exod. 15:20-21). And we remember that she follows Hannah who prayed, "The bows of the mighty are broken, but the feeble gird on strength" (1 Sam. 2:4). After receiving her blessing from Elizabeth, Mary lifted her arms and voice and began to sing her canticle of love, hope, and freedom:

"My soul magnifies the Lord,
    and my spirit rejoices in God my Savior,
for he has looked with favor on the lowliness of his servant.
    Surely, from now on all generations will call me blessed;
for the Mighty One has done great things for me,

and holy is his name.
His mercy is for those who fear him
    from generation to generation.
He has shown strength with his arm;
    he has scattered the proud in the thoughts of their hearts.
He has brought down the powerful from their thrones,
    and lifted up the lowly;
he has filled the hungry with good things,
    and sent the rich away empty.
He helped his servant Israel,
    in remembrance of his mercy,
according to the promise he made to our ancestors,
    to Abraham and to his descendants forever."

Mary seems to have picked up the baton of deliverance from the Hebrew scriptures and passed it on to the world of the New Testament and beyond. Mary sang the Magnificat, her aria of hope and freedom, as if she were about to birth a revolution. E. Stanley Jones declared the Magnificat "the most revolutionary document in the world." It stands out as one of the great hymns of the church, set to music by Johann Sebastian Bach. The Magnificat continues the theme of deliverance and liberation found in the Exodus, echoing and projecting into the future the words, "Let my people go!" It evokes Jeremiah's revolutionary prophecy when he proclaimed that God had appointed him to "pluck up and break down" (Jer. 18:7).

Thirty years later, Jesus would appear as an itinerant, charismatic preacher echoing the same song. His inaugural sermon in the synagogue of his hometown of Nazareth reverberates with the theme of Mary's song:

The Spirit of the Lord is upon me,
    because he has anointed me to bring good news to the poor.
He has sent me to proclaim release to the captives
    and recovery of sight to the blind, to let the oppressed go free,
to proclaim the year of the Lord's favor.

                    —Luke 4:18-19

Jesus proclaimed this message throughout his ministry: "Blessed are the poor, blessed are the hungry, blessed are the peacemakers, blessed are the meek, blessed are those who mourn" (see Luke 6:20-21; Matt. 5:3-9).

Singing Mary's Song reminds us that if we as individuals or members of a congregation have lost sight of human sin, darkness, oppression, and poverty, then we will certainly miss the full impact of Jesus' birth.

1. Where did Jesus, God-With-Us, come to you today?
2. What challenges or barriers—emotional, spiritual, practical—prevented you from experiencing Advent today?
3. Who are (or have been) the Elizabeths of your life? For whom can you be an Elizabeth?
4. Miriam sang a song of praise when God freed the Israelites from slavery in Egypt. Mary sings a song of hope for deliverance of the lowly and the hungry. For whom do you hope for liberation and freedom?

Prayer: Thank you, God, for Mary's song of freedom and hope and for her leap of faith. Help us to pray as she prayed, "Here am I, the servant of the Lord; let it be with me according to your word." Amen.

TUESDAY

Jesus' Birth Brings Hope

SCRIPTURE READING • LUKE 1:56; 2:1-7

Mary remained with [Elizabeth] about three months and then returned to her home" (Luke 1:56). She left Elizabeth's warm embrace and came home to Joseph. What was going on in her mind as she waited the remaining five or six months of her pregnancy? She must have repeated time and time again the words she had spoken to the angel: "How can this be?" Like any expectant mother, she probably spent time thinking about her baby—wondering how delivery would go, what the child would look like, and whether it would be strong and healthy. She may have worried about herself and her own health. Did she hope the angel would appear again?

We have no record of any conversations between Mary and Joseph during these days. But they must have spent hours together contemplating their future. Picture Mary's visit with Elizabeth calming her fears as she grew to appreciate that, for whatever reason, God had chosen her. The words of her song were her personal words of faith and hope as well as a proclamation for the world.

After the emperor's decree ordering the census, Mary and Joseph made the long and difficult journey just in time; for no sooner had they arrived in Bethlehem than the labor of childbirth came upon Mary. But no elaborate preparations were made for this birth. It took place like any other amid the harsh conditions of the ancient world. God entered human history as a completely helpless newborn baby. Jesus' parents were average citizens and would soon become refugees.

This birth took place on a straw-covered dirt floor—no antiseptic labor room; no anesthesiologist; no crisp, clean linen for the bed. The aroma was that of animals herded into a stable on a cold night for warmth and protection.

Humble beginnings remain the stark reality for much of the world's population: a person in rural America giving birth alongside the road because the closest hospital was too far to reach in time, an illegal immigrant afraid to seek medical help, an unwed teenager giving birth without her family, or millions of poor women delivering children without the medical attention that they deserve. These all form a part of the family of God.

Think of those whose spirit has grown faint, as Mary and Joseph's might have that night: young soldiers, some leaving their families and uncertain about their futures and others returning with severe physical and mental wounds; a retired couple struggling to make ends meet, whose son and family need to move in because he has lost his job; a single parent who can barely drag herself out of bed in the morning because she feels so burned-out and used up; an elderly man who asks his pastor to pray that the Lord will take him.

How does Advent—the coming of Jesus—offer comfort to those who experience this type of pain? How does it offer comfort to you?

Jesus was born long ago in a Judean village, anonymous and mostly unnoticed. But the hope for today remains that Christ continues to come to the shadowy and barren places of our lives. This is the good news of Advent. In the Greco-Roman world for which Luke was writing his Gospel, describing a god in these kinds of loving, gracious, and caring terms would have been an almost unthinkable concept. The apostle Paul helps us comprehend the magnitude of Advent by declaring that in Christ, "All the fullness of God was pleased to dwell, and through him God was pleased to reconcile to himself all things" (Col. 1:19-20).

Mary's song brought hope to those in the first century and brings hope and a challenge to us today. The angel's parting words to Mary, "For nothing will be impossible with God" (Luke 1:37), echo the words God spoke to Sarah, "Is anything too wonderful for the LORD?" (Gen. 18:14). What seemed "impossible" for these two women had become reality. The same thought was the essence of Jesus' ministry: "What is impossible for mortals is possible for God" (Luke 18:27).

The unfolding drama of Jesus' life brims with impossibilities—a virgin conceives, and God enters human history; a woman well beyond childbearing years delivers a healthy child; a man returns to life from a tomb; the Holy Spirit empowers a small, frightened group of men and women huddled in an upper room in Jerusalem to develop into a worldwide movement that for twenty-one centuries has "been turning the world upside down" (Acts 17:6).

And we can be assured that we have not seen the last of God's mighty deeds, because the angel's promise to Mary is given in the future tense: "For nothing *will be* impossible with God" (emphasis added).

Singing Mary's Song reminds us that a new day is coming when "justice [will] roll down like waters, and righteousness like an ever-flowing stream" (Amos 5:24).

1. Where did Jesus, God-With-Us, come to you today?
2. What challenges or barriers—emotional, spiritual, practical—prevented you from experiencing Advent today?
3. With whom do you most identify in the story—Mary, a young, unmarried woman? Elizabeth, bearing a child late in life? Joseph, facing the judgment of his peers? What do you learn from their encounters with the messengers of God?
4. What impossible situation are you facing in life now?

5. Who has taught you, either by word or example, that nothing is impossible for God?

Prayer: Watchful God, keep us alert and awake as we wait. In our everyday, ordinary lives, help us to seek diligently and watch for signs of your coming around us. Nothing is impossible with you. May the birth of Christ occur not only in history but in us as well. Amen.

WEDNESDAY
How Beautiful the World Could Be
SCRIPTURE READING • LUKE 1:52-55

In the Magnificat (named for the opening word in the Latin translation), Mary praised God for the favor bestowed on her, God's handmaiden of low esteem, and anticipated and modeled what God will do for the impoverished masses of the world. When Mary sang, "He has brought down the powerful from their thrones, and lifted up the lowly," she revealed the complete reversal of fortunes that will accompany God's final triumph—the powerful and the rich will exchange places with the powerless and the poor.

Luke emphasized this theme of Mary's song through his Gospel and into the book of Acts. The parable of the rich man and Lazarus (Luke 16:19-31), included only in Luke, describes a wealthy person dressed in royal purple (the color of opulence, power, and position), who lived insulated from poverty, pain, and human misery. In Jesus' day people ate with their hands. In the wealthy households, they wiped their hands with chunks of bread and then cast the bread on the floor. So when we read that Lazarus "longed to satisfy his hunger with what fell from the rich man's table," the description should be taken literally. Lazarus's condition was such that he could not ward off the dogs that came and licked his sores. At death the character's positions reversed: the poor man was carried away by angels to dwell with Abraham; the rich man, tormented in Hades. The crowd listening to this parable must have been shocked by its conclusion.

Jesus' teaching conveyed a harsh judgment against those who use power and wealth to control others and ignore the pain of oppression and hopelessness; it also, like Mary, painted a picture of hope as to what the world could be. Viktor Frankl, who spent three years in the Nazi prison camp at Auschwitz, recalled one evening when he and his companions, already at rest following a difficult day, were called to witness a wonderful sunset.

> Standing outside we saw sinister clouds glowing in the west and the whole sky alive with clouds of ever-changing shapes and colors, from steel blue to blood red. The desolate grey mud huts provided a sharp contrast, while the puddles on the muddy ground reflected the glowing sky. Then, after minutes of moving silence, one prisoner said to another, "How beautiful the world *could* be!"[1]

Most of us cannot escape the dark side of life as easily as the rich man in Jesus' parable. The media bombards us relentlessly with accounts of crime, drought, famine, civil wars, the plight of refugees, and economic recession. At the same time, we lose track of how beautiful the world can be. Advent provides that reminder. Advent promises us that a new world order is coming. Christ has come to pick up the fragmented pieces of our lives and, in his healing hands, make those lives whole and meaningful again.

A colleague who had undergone severe financial reversals once said to me, "I have experienced the love of God and the support of friends in a way that I could never before have imagined." From a financial perspective, he had lost much; but in the process he had learned the true meaning of friends, love, prayer, and worship and had come to realize how beautiful life could be. Life does not depend on money. My colleague now reaches out to others who suffer the pain and defeat he has known, having discovered a sense of meaning and purpose for his life that financial success could never provide.

The Advent message predicts a future of freedom and hope and also speaks to those of us who have food, education, and secure employment, revealing our need for release from the stranglehold of a lifestyle in which our possessions control us. It speaks deliverance to those in poverty as well. Jesus lives among us to bring the hope of freedom to everyone who seeks deliverance from oppression and bondage, to those who have much and those who have nothing.

The Advent hymn "Good Christian Friends, Rejoice" states, "Jesus Christ was born for this!" This Christmas will not be the same for anyone

- who has lost a lifelong companion: "Jesus Christ was born for this!"
- who is keeping a faithful vigil at the bedside of a loved one for whom the future appears dark and uncertain: "Jesus Christ was born for this!"
- who is experiencing the deterioration of a relationship within a family or marriage: "Jesus Christ was born for this!"
- who is burdened by the pain and hurt of abusiveness or abandonment: "Jesus Christ was born for this!"

The message of Advent is that, whatever our circumstance in life, Jesus Christ was born to be with us wherever we are.

Good Christian friends, rejoice
with heart and soul and voice. . . .
[Christ] hath opened heaven's door,
and ye are blest forevermore,
Christ was born for this!
(UMH 224)

Singing Mary's Song reminds us how beautiful the world could be.

1. Where did Jesus, God-With-Us, come to you today?
2. What challenges or barriers—emotional, spiritual, practical—prevented you from experiencing Advent today?
3. Where do you see beauty? Where do you long for beauty?
4. Mary saw her pregnancy as a part of God's plan of salvation for the world. An ordinary girl, living an ordinary life, contributing to the extraordinary. How does your life contribute to the extraordinary grace of God in the world?
5. "Jesus Christ was born for this!" What situation, person, or place comes to mind when you hear this promise?

Prayer: Dear God, thank you for the gift you have given to us in Jesus. Help us to remain constantly aware of the new possibilities for life and living that he brings to us. Open our hearts to your spirit that we might show others how beautiful the world could be. Amen.

———— ❧ ————

THURSDAY

Believing in God's Presence and Power

SCRIPTURE READING • LUKE 1:57-79

W e do not easily accept the fact that God actually enters directly into our world or our lives. Even those whom God chooses as vessels of hope often meet God with skepticism. Zechariah, a priest from the order of Abijah (1 Chron. 24:10), and his wife, Elizabeth (Mary's relative, who also came from a priestly family), are described as "blameless" and "righteous" (KJV); in other words, they were faithful to the covenant and the law. But Elizabeth was barren, and the couple was advanced in years. Their situation recalls those of Abraham and Sarah, Isaac and Rebekah, Jacob and Rachel, and Hannah and Elkanah. And like them, Zechariah and Elizabeth had been praying for a child. One day Zechariah, in his function as a priest, entered the sanctuary to offer incense on behalf of the people waiting outside. As Zechariah stood at the altar, an angel appeared to him and he was "terrified; and fear overwhelmed him" (Luke 1:12). The angel said to him, "Do not be afraid Zechariah, for your prayer has been heard. Your wife Elizabeth will bear you a son, and you will name him John" (Luke 1:13).

Zechariah answered him emphatically, "I am an old man" (Luke 1:18). Just as swiftly and emphatically the angel retorted, "I am Gabriel" (Luke 1:19).

This reminds me of a story recounted by a sailor taking part in a training mission on a battleship.[2] Patchy fog was making visibility poor, and shortly after dark the lookout cried out, "Light on the starboard bow."

"Steady or moving?" the captain asked.

"Steady sir." The sailor knew the ship was on a collision course.

The captain ordered the signalman to signal the message, "We are on a collision course. Advise you to change course."

The return signal countered, "Advise you to change course."

Immediately the captain replied, "I'm the captain. Change course."

The answer came back, "I am a seaman second class. You'd better change course."

The furious captain shouted, "I'm a battleship. Change course!"

The answer: "I am a lighthouse."

The captain got the message, and the ship changed course.

When Zechariah abruptly and emphatically responded to Gabriel, "I am old!" and Gabriel just as emphatically replied, "I am Gabriel!" Zechariah got the message. Sadly, a priest who offered prayers and incense in the sanctuary was not prepared for God's direct intervention in answer to his prayer. When Gabriel announced to Zechariah that he came to bring good news, Zechariah did not believe him. (Zechariah's unbelief stands in marked contrast to Elizabeth's joyful expectation.) So the angel struck him speechless until the time of the child's birth.

During the months he spent speechless, Zechariah had time to pray and think about this intervention from on high in his life. We do not know what happened to Zechariah during this quiet interlude, but we can imagine that he did some serious soul-searching. When the angel's gag order was lifted, Zechariah spoke with a different attitude and delivered an inspiring prophecy:

> "By the tender mercy of our God,
> the dawn from on high will break upon us,
> to give light to those who sit in darkness and in the shadow of death,
> to guide our feet into the way of peace."

Zechariah's song of praise would be known to the Christian world as the Benedictus, named for the first word in the Latin text.

What a remarkable change had taken place in Zechariah. Although he had displayed an instant of hesitation, he now knew who he was and what he must do.

In 1939, a group of laypeople in the Netherlands approached their professor, Dutch theologian Hendrik Kraemer, and said, "Dr. Kraemer, some of our Jewish friends are disappearing, and we don't know what to do. Tell us what to do."

Kraemer answered, "I cannot tell you what to do, but I can tell you who you are. If you know who you are, you will know what to do." The laypeople subsequently organized the Dutch Resistance Movement.

When you are tempted to be less than what God has intended you to be, remember who you are and you will know what to do.

Singing Mary's Song reminds us of our calling and to whom we belong.

1. Where did Jesus, God-With-Us, come to you today?
2. What challenges or barriers—emotional, spiritual, practical—prevented you from experiencing Advent today?
3. When confronted by the angel, Zechariah said, "I am an old man." How do you define yourself? "I am [young, old, blind, fully employed, unemployed, a parent, a student]." How do you see your self-identity as a limitation? How might God see it as an opportunity?
4. Do you tend to receive God's entering into your life with disbelief (like Zechariah) or with joy (like Elizabeth)?
5. How do you deal with the skepticism of the world? Do you contribute to it? Ignore it? In what ways might you counter skepticism with hope?

Prayer: Dear Lord, when you seek to enter our lives, help us always to remain ready to see and to do your will. Open our eyes and ears to the message you have for us. Illumine us and calm us so that trust and obedience will take the place of our fears. Amen.

FRIDAY
Trusting God's Promises
SCRIPTURE READING • LUKE 2:22-39

The Gospel of Luke emphasizes that Jesus was born into a faithful Jewish family that meticulously observed the law. (Luke relates a number of instances when Jesus' parents did everything that the law required regarding their infant son.) Every Jewish boy was to be circumcised on the eighth day following his birth; so Joseph and Mary dutifully fulfilled this rite. A child also received his or her name at this time; Luke carefully points out that Jesus was given the name that had been revealed by the angel of the Lord to Mary at the Annunciation.

Devout parents of newborns had two other acts that were performed at the Temple in the following weeks: the redemption of the firstborn (when appropriate) and the purification of the mother. The act of redemption required paying the priest five shekels (Num. 18:15-16). The purification of the mother required a lamb and a pigeon or turtledove for an offering or, if the family could not afford a lamb, two turtledoves or pigeons (Lev. 12:1-8). This "offering of the poor" was what Mary and Joseph presented, a reminder that Jesus was born into a poor family from a remote village of Judea. I believe that Jesus had his widowed mother in mind when telling the parable about the woman who lost the coin (Luke 15:8-10), recalling a time when every penny was precious in their home. "Rejoice with me, for I have found the coin that I had lost" (15:9).

At the Temple the family met an old man named Simeon. The Holy Spirit had revealed to Simeon that he would not die until he had seen the Messiah. When he saw Jesus, Simeon took the infant in his arms and praised God saying,

> "Master, now you are dismissing your servant in peace,
>   according to your word;
> for my eyes have seen your salvation,
>   which you have prepared in the presence of all peoples,
> a light for revelation to the Gentiles
>   and for glory to your people Israel."

Simeon's song, called the Nunc Dimittis, forms the third great universal hymn of the church in Luke's birth narrative. After reciting these words, Simeon turned to Mary and said, "This child is destined for the falling and the rising of many in Israel . . . and a sword will pierce your own soul too."

One wonders if Mary realized the significance of Simeon's words. Although Luke tells us that "Mary treasured all of these words and pondered them in her heart" (Luke 2:19), it is possible she did not fully grasp the magnitude of Simeon's words until mourning her son's death. Picture Mary standing at the foot of the cross thirty years after this encounter, her thoughts drifting back to her teenage self, young and frightened; to the stable and the smell of hay and animals; and to the harsh conditions in which in her son had been born. I wonder what profession Mary had wanted her son to pursue? a carpenter like his father? a rabbi? She clearly seemed unprepared for what Jesus had become and for the outcome that resulted.

At the foot of the cross, Mary suffered the deepest loss a parent can know—the death of a child. How did she endure? She was not mentioned as one of the women who came to the tomb on Easter morning. Perhaps it all proved too painful.

Scripture records so little regarding Mary's life that any suppositions on our part can only be conjecture. The narrative of Jesus' birth emphasized her willing support of and obedience to God's plan. Perhaps she recalled the words of the angel to her at the time of her Annunciation, "Do not be afraid, Mary, for you have found favor with God" (Luke 1:30). In that moment she had responded, "Here am I, the servant of the Lord; let it be with me according to your word" (Luke 1:38). She had believed God's promise then and remembered how God had brought her through the events since. After all, the angel had also said, "For nothing will be impossible with God" (Luke 1:37). I believe that at the cross Mary felt the same conviction—that God was with her and would see her through.

Like Mary, there will be periods when our commitment, love, devotion, and faith are challenged and the promises of God remain all we have to stand on. Difficult times may cause us to doubt that God really is trustworthy. Prolonged illness and hurting can make God seem distant and uncaring. Sometimes God's delays appear to us as God's denial. But like Mary, we can look back and declare, "God was there all the time, and I never knew it." We can trust God's promises.

Singing Mary's Song reminds us that Advent is a time of waiting. The whole world is waiting, waiting for peace with justice, for freedom, for deliverance, for food, for redemption, and for reconciliation. The world waits. The Messiah comes.

1. Where did Jesus, God-With-Us, come to you today?
2. What challenges or barriers—emotional, spiritual, practical—prevented you from experiencing Advent today?
3. What promises or wisdom do you stand on? Quips from grandparents, family rules from childhood, scripture that has gotten you through difficult times?
4. Imagine yourself at the foot of the cross remembering the account of Jesus' birth. What stands out to you? What becomes more or less important in this hindsight?
5. As you prepare to celebrate the coming of the Christ child, what lessons from his humble beginnings will you carry with you in the coming weeks?

Prayer: O God, be our Refuge amid despair, be our Guide through everything dark and fearful, be our Guard against whatever threatens our spiritual well-being. Be our Strength in our stress and pain. Gladden our hearts with your peace; through Jesus Christ our Lord. Amen.

SATURDAY

Trusting God in the Messiness

SCRIPTURE READING • MATTHEW 1:18-25

Joseph, the father of Jesus, appears almost as an afterthought in the Christmas story. Mary receives top billing. Luke barely mentions Joseph; and although Matthew's account gives Joseph a more central role, Joseph still does not speak any lines. Look in your hymnal to see if you can find a single carol in which Joseph plays anything more than a bit part. Centuries of religious art have produced numerous "Madonna with infant" scenes, often with no sign of

Joseph (as though he were cropped out of the family portrait). In the numerous nativity scenes that decorate the base of our Christmas trees or fireplace mantels, Joseph often seems like little more than another bystander among the cows, sheep, wise men, and shepherds.

In reading the birth story in Matthew, we learn that Joseph and Mary were engaged (1:18), which in first-century Jewish culture meant they were already considered husband and wife. Therefore, unfaithfulness constituted adultery. So when Joseph became aware that Mary was pregnant, he decided to break off their relationship.

Matthew designates Joseph as a "righteous man" (1:19), a person utterly devoted to keeping the law and the covenant. As such he was legally justified to end their engagement. But Joseph's concern for the woman he loved caused him to temper his decision with mercy, since he knew what could happen to Mary if he divorced her because of infidelity. She might be killed or turned out by her family and ostracized by the community. She would have to scratch out an existence for herself and her child by begging, borrowing, or stealing. As a righteous man, Joseph would never want this for his family. Torn between loyalty to his wife and loyalty to the law, he attempted to honor both by deciding "to dismiss her quietly."

Joseph could not have understood the magnitude of his decision and its cosmic consequences, but an angel of the Lord appeared to him in a dream and said, "Joseph, son of David, do not be afraid to take Mary as your wife, for the child conceived in her is from the Holy Spirit. She will bear a son, and you are to name him Jesus, for he will save his people from their sins."

Joseph awoke willing to obey the startling and unexpected command of God and to put aside his decision in light of this word he heard from on high. We should not underestimate what a courageous act this was on Joseph's part. He probably felt that his whole future had fallen apart, that his good name had been dishonored, and (most disappointing of all) that his trust had been violated. Joseph could have simply walked away from this entire situation. But he did not. And although faced with a life he had not planned, he trusted God to work in the midst of his shattered dreams. Life turned out to be far more than Joseph had ever dreamed it could be.

Joseph's minor role establishes him as a human being of remarkable spiritual stature. He possessed the boldness, courage, daring, and strength of character to defy the expectations of his entire community and take Mary as his wife. He did so in spite of people who may have wanted to stone her for adultery. It may have been Joseph's vision of justice and mercy and obedience that prevented that outcome. Joseph directed his disappointment toward grace.

Joseph and Mary immediately were caught up in a whirlwind of events—forced to leave Nazareth and to travel more than eighty miles over rough terrain to Bethlehem, then to flee to Egypt as refugees when a decree by Herod threatened the life of their son. We can imagine Joseph providing protection and care for his family amid the difficulties.

Perhaps you can recollect a time when circumstances altered the future you had planned, steering you to a life you did not envision or desire. Joseph has left us with a clear witness:

> Here is a righteous man who surveys a mess he has had absolutely nothing to do with creating and decides to believe that God is present in it. With every reason to disown it all, to walk away from it in search of a neater, more controlled life with an easier, more conventional wife, Joseph does not do that. He claims the scandal, he owns the mess—he legitimizes it—and the mess becomes the place where the Messiah is born.[3]

When we accept the challenge to follow the will of God, we never know where life will lead us. We can be sure that it will probably never be dull. Just ask Joseph.

Singing Mary's Song reminds us that in spite of the unexpected twists and turns of life that may come our way, every low valley shall be exalted, every mountain will be made low, and every crooked path will be made straight (see Isa. 40:4).

1. Where did Jesus, God-With-Us, come to you today?
2. What challenges or barriers—emotional, spiritual, practical—prevented you from experiencing Advent today?

Prayer: O Lord, what do we do when life seems to cast us aside and we find ourselves immersed in circumstances that we did not choose and we cannot change? Our only hope is your promise, which you gave to your apostle under similar conditions, "My grace is sufficient for you." Lord, help us to believe. Amen.

WRITING YOUR MAGNIFICAT

During Advent, take time to write your own Magnificat. This week write the first verse. Use these questions to guide your work.

- How does your soul magnify the Lord?
- What do you know in the depths of your soul?
- Write a couplet about your fears right now.
- Write a couplet about uncovering hope in your fears.
- Write a couplet about overcoming the impossible.

WEEK 2: IN THE FULLNESS OF TIME

MARY SINGS

*"The Mighty One has done
great things for me."*

LUKE 1:49

THEME

Jesus was born at God's appointed time.

SUNDAY

In the Fullness of Time

SCRIPTURE READING • GALATIANS 4:4

The apostle Paul wrote, "When the fullness of time had come, God sent his Son, born of a woman, born under the law" (Gal. 4:4). Paul's words suggest that God had a definite goal, that all creation moved on a divine agenda, and that Jesus appeared at God's chosen time. Church theologians point out that Jesus came in the "fullness of time," when God made a new beginning and people began to enjoy a richer and fuller life. Paul described the ultimate aim of divine grace as "in Christ God was reconciling the world to himself" (2 Cor. 5:19).

But Christ's coming required preparation. One thing remains clear; God took the initiative. Because human beings are unable to go where God dwells, God has to come to where we are. We meet God in the midst of our hopes and fears, in our loves and hates, and in the joys of victory and the depths of defeat. In these God is manifested as the One who acts for us in history.

In many respects, God acted at an opportune time to break into human history and to bring the promised moment of redemption. A number of historical factors converged at the time that allowed the Christ event to unfold and Christianity to spread. First, the *Pax Romana* (peace of Rome) created a peaceful atmosphere that allowed the distribution of ideas throughout the Roman Empire. In this setting Jesus grew to adulthood, and his message spread rapidly throughout Judea and beyond. The peace achieved by the Romans endured for two centuries. Never before had the shores of the Mediterranean been as peaceful or enjoyed so much prosperity. In addition, the Romans were master road builders. Highways of solid construction traversed the empire, making travel and trade easier, safer, and more extensive than ever. Koiné Greek (the language of the New Testament) was spoken throughout the realm, with large Greek-speaking populations in Palestine, Egypt, Italy, and Rome. The Romans had also developed a highly efficient postal system.

Finally, the kingdom of Judea, where Jesus was born and spent his life, was no out-of-the-way country, cut off from the currents of the time, but lay at the heart of the overland trade network linking several centers of civilization—Egypt to the south, Rome to the west, and Mesopotamia to the east. Roman armies and heavily laden merchant caravans regularly marched through this crossroad of the ancient world. Merchants traveling north and south through Judea reported events, told stories, and shared their culture with the merchants and populace of Palestine. No doubt early Christians related stories of their newfound faith with these travelers, who took them back to their towns and cities far beyond Israel.

But at the same time, some people in the Jewish community thought that God had abandoned them or that God was unconcerned and withdrawn. No prophetic voice had been heard in the land for nearly three centuries, but the words of the Hebrew prophets that promised the coming of a messiah still burned in their hearts. Perhaps the cry of desperation recorded in the book of Isaiah was their cry as well: "O that you would tear open the heavens and come down" (64:1). Throughout these years of divine silence, there were those who still believed.

Then, in the Judean hill country, in "the fullness of time," the angel Gabriel visited a teenage Jewish girl in Nazareth and said to her, "Greetings, favored one! The Lord is with you" (Luke 1:28). After years of prophetic silence, at the opportune moment, Mary stepped onto the stage and fulfilled her call in the messianic promise. Mary stood at the intersection between the old and the new as she sang her aria of deliverance and hope. She was called blessed, for God had accorded her a remarkable distinction—to prepare God's Son for the world (thus her description as *Theotokos*, "mother of God").

One notable thing about Paul's claim in Galatians is that "in the fullness of time" God sent Jesus. Prior to the coming of Christ, humans tended to expect their experience of God to be distant or removed: For the psalmist, knowledge of God might be found in nature (see Psalms 8; 19; 104). For the nation of Israel, knowledge of God came through God's mighty acts of salvation in history. But in Christ, God came to earth clothed in human flesh. Those who encountered Jesus could claim to have seen God with their eyes. The writer of First John declares "We have seen with our eyes . . . and touched with our hands . . . the word of life" (1 John 1:1). The God who seemed so distant has come near. John affirms that if you want to see what this creating Word, this dynamic power, this controlling reason looks like—look to Jesus of Nazareth. "In him was life, and the life was the light of all people" (John 1:4). These words contain not only a basic truth but also a mystery. It is difficult for us to accept the fact that God is so down-to-earth, that God should come to us on such human and ordinary terms. We are astonished at God's availability.

Why is this claim so important? Because in our experiences of pain, disappointment, death, sorrow, rejection, failure, anguish, fear, anxiety, loneliness, and hopelessness, when we come to God in prayer with burdened hearts, we can say, "Lord, you know how we feel." God does, because the Word became flesh and lived among us "full of grace and truth."

Singing Mary's Song reminds us that the basic word for Advent is Immanuel, "God is with us."

1. Where did Jesus, God-With-Us, come to you today?
2. What challenges or barriers—emotional, spiritual, practical—prevented you from experiencing Advent today?
3. What does it mean that God has taken the initiative in history? How has God taken the initiative in your life? How will you respond?
4. Write, draw, or consider the time line of your life. Where do you see God's perfect timing in your own life?

5. What thought, if any, have you given to the historical Jesus? How do these insights about geography, politics, and culture support, enhance, or challenge how you will observe Advent this year?

Prayer: O Lord, grant to us in these troubling days a clearer vision of your truth, a greater faith in your power, and a more confident assurance in your love. Amen.

MONDAY

The Word Became Flesh

SCRIPTURE READING • JOHN 1:1-14

Galatians 4:4 not only suggests God's timetable regarding the "fullness of time" but also reveals important factors relating to the human nature of Jesus. Jesus was flesh and bone like us and lived his life in complete solidarity with us. Jesus was vulnerable to the conditions of human life, though he did not sin—a fact that New Testament writers mention repeatedly (Acts 3:14; 2 Cor. 5:21; Heb. 4:15; 5:9; 7:26; 1 Pet. 2:22; 1 John 3:5).

We have a hard time understanding the doctrine of the Incarnation—Jesus becoming fully human. Many people have asked how Jesus could have been both human and divine. Where does the one begin and the other end? These questions arise because in many New Testament stories Jesus performed supernatural acts (such as miracles and foreknowledge of the future) but in others displayed specifically human traits.

The Gospel of John describes Jesus' Incarnation by saying, "The Word became flesh and lived among us, . . . full of grace and truth." Although the church has never been able to explain fully the mystery of how Jesus can be both human and divine, church doctrine affirms that he is both.

Mary served not merely as the point of Jesus' entrance into the world. As his mother, she cared for his physical, mental, and spiritual needs. She nursed him, nurtured him, and taught him the ways of the Lord. Doubtless, she taught him to memorize the psalms and to pray.

One thing remains certain regarding Jesus' having been born of a human mother: he was fully human and underwent the consequences that entailed. Jesus felt every human need and appetite—hunger, thirst, exhaustion, suffering, sorrow, and death. Jesus had limited knowledge and had to grow in wisdom and stature (Luke 2:52, KJV). Physically, intellectually, emotionally, and spiritually, Jesus lived the same life each of us lives. He prayed to God for the same reasons we pray.

Before beginning his public ministry, Jesus faced severe temptation (see Luke 4:1-14). His time of testing caused not only physical pain (given the brutal conditions in the desert) but also emotional pain as he confronted the temptation to use his gifts and powers for himself. Jesus faced sorrow and grief throughout his ministry as well, being constantly exposed to the hunger, pain, and suffering in the lives of others. Scripture tells us that when he looked at the crowds he had "compassion for them" (Matt. 14:14). And Jesus lived through sorrow and grief in his personal relationships as well. Jesus wept after his friend Lazarus had died (John 11:35). Jesus' tears were a public acknowledgment of the difficulties that death causes in human life.

George Buttrick reminds us that

> Christ was fashioned as we are. Like us he was weary at night-fall; his tears were salty like ours; and when he cut his hand, his blood was red and crimson like our blood. He was a tradesman, who labored in his father's carpenter shop, knew firsthand about irritable customers, and during hard times found it hard to collect his bills and make ends meet. He craved human friendship. He identified with the undesirables and grieved over the stubbornness of men. He knew the plight of the poor and the shame of the outcast. He laughed with little children and shared the anguish of parents who sorrowed over the death of a child. He suffered the despair of the unemployed in the marketplace. He died bleeding, but not before he also felt our ultimate doubt, "My God, my God, why have you forsaken me?" He was "crucified, dead, and buried"—a phrase that encapsulates the creed's

blunt statement of his humanness. He was of the good earth. That he fully partook of our life there is no doubt.[1]

Paul declared that Jesus was "born of a woman" (Gal. 4:4), revealing how Jesus' dramatic birth accomplished the radical entry of God into our world and into our daily lives. Jesus' coming into our world of political unrest, war, severe economic recession, famine, natural disaster, and unrelenting pain and sorrow provides us hope. Every time we repeat the creed, "I believe . . . in Jesus Christ his only Son our Lord . . . who was born of the Virgin Mary," we affirm that Jesus is at once fully human and fully God.

The theme of Advent is "God is with us." God came to earth and thus identified the Divine self with the causes of humanity. God did not come into the world as an angel or a superhuman spirit but as a human being. In doing so, God put the divine stamp of approval on human life. God not only comes to stand with us but to deliver us and lead us out to a new life, to a new beginning of hope and freedom.

What does the Incarnation teach us about God?

- *That God knows.* God is present in our struggles and failures.
- *That God hears.* God is open to our cries.
- *That God heals.* "Come to me, all you that are weary and are carrying heavy burdens, and I will give you rest" (Matt. 11:28).

Singing Mary's Song reminds us that God has come among us and knows every aspect of our lives and living. Truly the Word has become human flesh and blood and lives among us full of grace and truth.

1. Where did Jesus, God-With-Us, come to you today?
2. What challenges or barriers—emotional, spiritual, practical—prevented you from experiencing Advent today?
3. Jesus' Incarnation is a mystery—he was fully human and fully divine. Talk with Jesus the Human One about a struggle that you are having. Now talk with Jesus, the divine Son of God, concerning the same struggle. What wisdom did you gain from both conversations?
4. As humans, can we become all compassion? What can we learn from God's unbounded love?

Prayer: O God, keep us mindful that you took on our human nature so that we might take on divine ways, especially in our love for others. Equip us to serve you in the spirit and power of Christ. Let your presence flow through us. Amen.

TUESDAY

Ordinary Folks Living Extraordinary Lives

SCRIPTURE READING • LUKE 4:16-30

Sometimes God comes to us in the ordinary routine of life's activities, which may be why Jesus' neighbors had a hard time accepting him once he started his public ministry. He had returned from his soul-wrenching temptation in the desert and come home to Nazareth. "As was his custom," he went to the synagogue on the sabbath. It seems fitting that Jesus would preach his first sermon in the town where he grew up. He selected a text from the book of Isaiah, a passage that would characterize the nature of his ministry: "The Spirit of the Lord is upon me . . . to bring good news to the poor." Jesus read the text, handed the scroll back to the attendant, sat down, and said to the expectant crowd, "Today this scripture has been fulfilled in your hearing."

Luke tells us, "All spoke well of him and were amazed at the gracious words that came from his mouth." When a new celebrity returns home, the crowd is often complimentary, and the congregation in Nazareth was no different. Many people spoke words of appreciation for Jesus that day.

But then Jesus gave a two-point discourse and the mood began to shift: Elijah, he said, was sent by God to obtain help from a non-Jewish, foreign woman, a widow in Zarephath (see 1 Kings 17); and Elisha had healed the leper Naaman, a foreigner from Syria, but had not healed any Israelites who had leprosy (2 Kings 5). After Jesus had spoken, "all in the synagogue were filled with rage." Jesus' first sermon was not particularly well received. Why did his sermon cause so much trouble?

Perhaps the answer lies in that the Jewish congregation, as members of the chosen people, believed they had a special claim on God; Jesus' words, however, implied that everyone, the Jewish community and those beyond, has a claim on God. Jesus' position challenged the congregation's exceptionalism and exclusiveness. They were so enraged that they drove Jesus out of town to the brow of a hill in order to hurl him off the cliff.

That day in Nazareth the people stumbled over the truth because it appeared so ordinary and familiar. Fred Craddock once related an incident about the death of a saint. Those who visited the saint's home after his death were astonished to see a broom, detergent, trash cans, an ironing board, dirty dishes, a worn sweater, toilet tissue, a can of tuna, old newspapers, artificial sweetener, and utility bills. With astonishment they gasped, "He was just like us!"

We find it difficult to realize and believe that God brings liberation to us on limping, human feet, through the most ordinary and the least expected means. At times the highest comes to us amid the lowest.

For one year I taught at the Methodist Theological Seminary in Ghana, West Africa, when my wife worked in the seminary library. On Saturdays we would visit the American Club at the American Embassy in Accra. The American Club served as a terminal for Peace Corps members going and coming from the United States. We always looked forward to meeting several of them each week and hearing their stories.

One Saturday we met a young woman who had graduated from the University of Minnesota as an agriculturalist the previous spring. She had been working in a village in the northern farm area of Ghana, helping the farmers establish a summer cash crop. But she had contracted malaria, which left her weak and tired, and was now heading home to get medical care and to visit her family. She had ridden for two days in the back of a pickup; the hot sun had bleached her hair; and she looked exhausted. She told us, however, that as soon as she could obtain proper medication, she planned to return for the spring planting.

When I asked why she had chosen this career, she replied, "You don't know what a difference this crop will mean to these farmers. It will provide them a livelihood. It gives their only hope of escape from debilitating poverty and famine."

The young woman went on to explain what this opportunity to serve others had meant to her. "I have found the most fulfilling thing in my life. This is what I have been called to do with my life at this time." Nothing could be more meaningful for her than to know her life was making a significant difference.

We never met that young woman again, but we talk about her often. Did she recover? Did she go back? We do not doubt that in her work she had discovered the highest purpose for her life in the most unexpected place. By giving herself to the poor, marginalized, and powerless people of the land, she had found her life. As she plans her future, I hope she remembers the power of that time and why it fulfilled her.

Jesus had something to say about losing one's life in order to find it (Matt. 10:39). Sometimes life's brightest moments are found lurking in what we consider the world's lowest places.

Singing Mary's Song reminds us that the greatest lesson in our life is knowing that we can make a difference.

1. Where did Jesus, God-With-Us, come to you today?
2. What challenges or barriers—emotional, spiritual, practical—prevented you from experiencing Advent today?
3. Recall a time when you encountered a saint—a person faithful, compassionate, and true. How did you feel in his or her presence? Based on that experience, contemplate what being in Jesus' presence might be like.
4. Identify a time when you sustained a loss only to discover that it allowed you to find new life.
5. Through what unexpected place, time, or person has God been revealed to you? What do you recall about that event or person?

Prayer: Dear God, help us to remain aware of your presence in all places at all times. Give us a more sensitive attitude toward others that we might see you in the unexpected. Help us to meet you there. Amen.

WEDNESDAY

Your Prayer Has Been Heard

SCRIPTURE READING • LUKE 1:5-17

Delays cause anxiety. Standing with a family in a hospital waiting room while a loved one undergoes emergency surgery can seem like an eternity. The family members sit quietly as the minutes drag into hours. They pray for a doctor or nurse to bring an encouraging word. As they silently look at one another, their eyes reflect their thoughts: *What will we do if he doesn't make it?* Some sit in small groups, holding hands and praying for the best, but bracing for the worst.

Zechariah had been waiting. As a direct descendent of Aaron, he was a priest; but in New Testament times Aaron's descendants had grown so numerous that their duties, including the burning of incense, were allocated by lot.[2] Every priest must have longed for the honor of participating in the worship ceremony in the Temple. On this day the lot fell to Zechariah. Think of his joy after waiting for what felt like an eternity for this opportunity of a lifetime.

But Zechariah had his own concerns and had been waiting for another reason. He and Elizabeth, his wife, were childless and beyond childbearing age. But now, as he stood at the altar, an angel informed him, "Do not be afraid, Zechariah, for your prayer has been heard. Your wife Elizabeth will bear you a son, and you will name him John. You will have joy and gladness, and many will rejoice at his birth." In what has been described as a "wordless daze of joy," Zechariah finished his Temple duties and hurried home to share the news with Elizabeth.

But when I think about delay, my thoughts again turn to Mary. Not regarding Jesus' birth, because those events moved quite rapidly. In fact, it probably proved to be a rather hectic period: her visit with Elizabeth; the birth in Bethlehem; the visit of the shepherds; Jesus' circumcision; the journey to the Temple for Mary's act of purification; and, ultimately, the family's flight to Egypt. To me the amazing part in all this activity was the ease with which Mary believed and welcomed everything that God was accomplishing in and through her life.

God's intervention in the lives of biblical characters, as well as their responses, varied widely. Sarah laughed when she overheard God's plan for her and Abraham, her ninety-nine-year-old husband. Moses tried to convince God that God had the wrong person, that he (Moses) did not fit the job description and lacked communication skills. Gideon complained that his resources were inadequate. Isaiah doubted he was righteous enough to do God's work. Jonah jumped ship and fled in the opposite direction.

But Mary's reaction differed from all the others. She simply believed God. Without hesitation she accepted God's call. Her response exemplified her courageous faith: "Here am I, the servant of the Lord; let it be with me according to your word" (Luke 1:38).

Following the chaotic months surrounding Jesus' birth, delay became an important aspect of Mary's life. After the family returned from Egypt and settled down in Nazareth, the biblical account falls nearly silent concerning the next thirty years. Imagine Mary remembering the angel telling her, "[Jesus] will be great, and will be called the Son of the Most High, and the Lord God will give to him the throne of his ancestor David" (Luke 1:32) but wondering, during these many years in Nazareth when life turned out to be rather domestic, when this prediction would come true. These "silent" years must have been hard for her.

What do we do when our plans do not work out as we have prayed and hoped? John Claypool provides insight about his struggle and agony after being informed that his eight-year-old daughter was suffering from lymphatic leukemia and had only eighteen months to live.[3] Claypool writes that his whole world turned upside down. The day she died, he said, "will always be the saddest day of my life." During those times of earnest prayer and anxious waiting, no miraculous healing or divine intervention arrived. Instead, God sustained him through what he called "the gift of endurance." He found himself upheld by God's words to Paul, "My grace is sufficient for you, for power is made perfect in weakness" (2 Cor. 12:9). Claypool learned that what saw him through was not God's intervention with instant healing but rather the sustaining presence of God's grace. "In more than forty years in the parish ministry I have lived through miraculous growth in a faith that was willing to put total trust in God when a miraculous answer to prayer was obviously not forthcoming."

After many years in parish ministry, I also have discovered that more people are sustained by "the gift of endurance" than are visited by instantaneous, miraculous healings.

Another biblical example of the gift of endurance would be Paul's struggle with what he described as "a thorn . . . in the flesh" (see 2 Cor. 12:7-10). No one knows what his thorn was, but he prayed three times for relief. God answered his prayer by saying, "My grace is sufficient for you." God answered Paul's prayer, just not in the manner Paul expected. Although he carried the thorn to his grave, in the process Paul grew in stature and faith as an apostle of Jesus Christ.

Mary endured those long, silent years in Nazareth as her son grew into adulthood. Then came "The voice of one crying out in the wilderness: 'Prepare the way of the Lord'" (Luke 3:4). She realized that Jesus' time had arrived. It was a long time coming, but I believe that Mary again "treasured all these words and pondered them in her heart" (Luke 2:19). Like Zechariah's, Mary's time of waiting had come to an end.

Singing Mary's Song reminds us to pray patiently, knowing that grace and hope will prevail and a new day of justice is coming.

1. Where did Jesus, God-With-Us, come to you today?
2. What challenges or barriers—emotional, spiritual, practical—prevented you from experiencing Advent today?
3. What are your physical responses to waiting? Do you feel annoyed? angry? a tightness in your chest? a headache? exhaustion? Envision that God is present with you in the waiting, and release and relax your physical body.
4. Picture again the time line of your life. Have you gone through weeks, months, or years when God seemed silent? Where was God? Why couldn't you hear God?
5. Do you see endurance (long-suffering) as a gift? How is endurance linked to grace?

Prayer: Lord, when there is no answer or no immediate way out, give us the gift of endurance through your grace that we may be patient in our hope. Amen.

THURSDAY

Love Was Born at Christmas

SCRIPTURE READING • PSALM 23

The Bible recounts the unfolding drama of God's activity in human life, providing a unity that moves from the Creation in Genesis to the new creation with the birth of Christ. Like any great drama, it deals with people's hopes and fears, their joys and their anguish, their ambitions and their failures. But this drama is unique, because God the Director not only stands behind the scenes prompting and directing the drama but also appears as a member of the cast. In fact, at the climactic instant, in the birth of Jesus, God stepped onto the world stage as the protagonist. When Mary sings about "lifting up the lowly" and "filling the hungry with good things," she introduces words of love that set the theme for the plot.

When I first met Johnny, he was dying of lung cancer. He had just received word that he had only a few months to live and had been placed under hospice care. Johnny was a poor, frightened man sent home to die in the only home he knew—an ancient, singlewide trailer in a rundown trailer park. He suffered not just from the ravages of cancer but also from the effects of racism, poverty, and the lack of human kindness. I worked with the hospice staff to provide pastoral care for Johnny. As the weeks passed, we developed into a well-coordinated team—the nurse, a family-support counselor, a music therapist, and me.

My relationship with Johnny deepened, and we built trust over time as he related his life's journey to me. In the late 1940s, he left elementary school to help his family with the chores on their sharecropper's farm. As he grew older the only work he could find was logging in the pine forest around Tallahassee, where he toiled for nearly thirty years. During that time, he never made more than seven dollars an hour; had no benefits like workmen's compensation or health insurance; and was always paid in cash, so he had never filed a tax return and was ineligible for Social Security. He grew older and weaker and, when he reached the point that he could no longer handle a chain saw or climbing, the company let him go.

As Johnny shared these incidents with me, I could sense how difficult life was for a poor, uneducated black man growing up in rural north Florida in the mid-1900s. Johnny was not bitter; in fact he remained an outgoing and jovial man, grateful for everything we did for him. He grew on all of us. He also grew weaker until he was bedridden. When I asked him if he knew what was happening, he replied, "Yes. I am dying." We had discussed his death earlier, but it had seemed far off at the time. "I am afraid," Johnny said, "because I don't know what to expect."

In our moments together we had honest, open discussions regarding death, dying, and God. Although Johnny felt unworthy because he had not attended church since he was a child, I assured him he did not have to earn God's love, that God loved him regardless. Over his last several weeks, we repeatedly read his favorite scripture, the Twenty-third Psalm. Each time I came to visit, he would repeat his version of his favorite verse: "Even though I walk through the dark valley, God is with me. I am not afraid." I told him to hold on to this promise and it would see him through.

Johnny was special to me. As we talked at length, I sensed that I was standing on holy ground, listening to this man's soul. He had never been given this kind of care in his life: hospice volunteers brought in his favorite food, did housecleaning, and repaired his disintegrating trailer; the music therapist and he sang the songs he enjoyed most.

When Johnny's health was declining, we kept a faithful vigil by his bedside, determined to keep our promise that he would not die alone. The music therapist lightly strummed her guitar. As the nurse stood by his side making sure he was comfortable, he whispered to her, "You are so good." I held Johnny's weak, scarred, calloused hand and prayed, "The LORD bless you and keep you; the LORD make his face to shine upon you, and be gracious to you; the LORD lift up his countenance upon you, and give you peace" (Num. 6:24-26). The small group around his bed whispered softly, "Amen." Johnny's agitation and fear gave way to peace. This was probably the first time in a long while that he had felt that much loving support and care. Our attention turned toward something greater than ourselves, to the forgiveness, mercy, grace, and acceptance of a loving God.

Now during Advent, as I look back to that moment, I am reminded of Jesus' promise to the dying man on the cross next to him, "Today you will be with me in Paradise" (Luke 23:43). For "Love came down at Christmas, Love all lovely, Love divine" (UMH 242).

Singing Mary's Song reminds us that Jesus came among us to lift up the lowly, and that we are called to assist him in that task.

1. Where did Jesus, God-With-Us, come to you today?
2. What challenges or barriers—emotional, spiritual, practical—prevented you from experiencing Advent today?
3. "The Bible recounts the unfolding drama of God's activity in human life." What part are you called to play in this unfolding drama?
4. When has love been revealed to you in weakness, scars, and callouses?

Prayer: Thank you, Lord, for your love so deep, so high, and so broad. There is no place we can go that is out of bounds of your love and care. Help us not to forget that our greatest opportunity is sharing that good news with others. Amen.

FRIDAY

For the People Have Walked in Darkness

SCRIPTURE READING • LUKE 7:18-23

John the Baptist represents a key character in the Advent account. In a sense, he functions as the last character of the Old Testament. Luke 7:18-19 provides an interesting lectionary text to consider at Advent: "John summoned two of his disciples and sent them to the Lord to ask, 'Are you the one who is to come, or are we to wait for another?'" Is it possible that John, the man who baptized Jesus, could be doubting his own message? Had John grown impatient because Jesus was not the messiah that John expected him to be?

For John, the ax was lying at the root of the tree and the winnowing process was taking place (Luke 3:9, 17; Matt. 3:12). For him, the fires of judgment had already started to burn. Perhaps John expected Jesus to act more like him—a fiery reformer and prophet of judgment and repentance. Maybe he was surprised that Jesus' ministry had taken a different course by emphasizing grace and healing. A man facing execution cannot afford to have doubts. So John sent his disciples to ask Jesus if "we should look for another."

John wanted to know when Jesus was going to "get on board," why he was so slow to declare that the day of God's holy destruction was at hand. Notice that Jesus' answer to John did not talk about impending judgment. Rather Jesus pointed out that "the blind receive their sight, the lame walk, the lepers are cleansed, the deaf hear, the dead are raised, the poor have good news brought to them." Jesus' answer to John reflects the whole gospel of good news. His answer fulfills the hopeful message of Advent in the words of the prophet Isaiah, "The people who walked in darkness have seen a great light; . . . on them light has shined" (9:2), and of Mary, "[God's] mercy is for those who fear him from generation to generation" (Luke 1:50).

Jesus' final words to John, "Blessed is anyone who takes no offense at me," suggest that John had only grasped half the truth about Jesus. John preached a gospel of judgment and destruction, whereas Jesus preached a gospel of deliverance from bondage through grace, defining grace as the love of God in action. Jesus seems to say to John, "Maybe I am not doing what you expect me to do, but the forces of evil are being defeated by the transforming force of love and grace and not by overwhelming power."

To some extent John's questions are our questions. John speaks for those who were once sure of their faith but are now uncertain. We wonder whether the way of diplomacy and non-retaliation can survive in a world where power resides in the hands of so few. Does God actually exist? Does God love and care for us? Does God have a plan for the world? for me? for my community? Is Jesus the definitive answer to these ultimate questions or should we look elsewhere? These are serious questions.

Bart D. Ehrman, a distinguished professor of religious studies and a leading authority on the history of the early church, surprised me with his book *God's Problem: How the Bible Fails to Answer Our Most Important Question—Why We*

Suffer. He describes his religious journey as having started as a committed and devout evangelical Christian; pursuing his education at the Moody Bible Institute, Wheaton College, and finally Princeton Theological Seminary, where he earned a PhD in biblical studies; and, ultimately, becoming a nonbeliever (a "happy agnostic"). He reached a point when he could no longer believe in a god who allowed such excruciating and unspeakable pain in the world. He could no longer reconcile the claims of faith with the facts of life. He no longer goes to church and no longer considers himself a Christian. Interestingly, he still teaches biblical studies. Ehrman took a step beyond that taken by John the Baptist—he didn't just wonder if he should look for someone else but actually decided to do so.

I remember vividly when a devastating earthquake struck Haiti on January 12, 2010. The early reports were that Port-au-Prince had been transformed into piles of rubble, and the death toll topped two hundred thousand. The pictures of the devastation were soul wrenching. I had participated in mission trips to Haiti and knew the poverty, so my first thoughts were, *O Lord, not Haiti!*

A *New York Times* headline read, "Haiti's Angry God!"[4] The article stated, "If God exists, he's really got it in for Haiti." In contrast, the article also reported that as darkness settled over the destruction, amid the crying and the pleas for help, the singing of hymns drifted over the city. The article related how a Haitian pastor stood atop the rubble of his church and tearfully gave an impromptu sermon, reassuring his listeners, "It seems like the Good Lord is hiding, but he's here. He's always here!"

Amid the kind of pain and death that had caused one colleague to lose his faith in God, these words of an unnamed Haitian pastor have captured the message of Advent: "It seems like the Good Lord is hiding, but he's here. He's always here!" Immanuel.

Singing Mary's Song reminds us of Immanuel, "God is with us," now and forevermore.

1. Where did Jesus, God-With-Us, come to you today?
2. What challenges or barriers—emotional, spiritual, practical—prevented you from experiencing Advent today?
3. John's question, "Are you the one?" remains our question. When have you asked this question? How has Jesus answered you?

4. Do you believe—in the depth of your soul—that God is always present? If not, what keeps you from believing? If so, what gives you assurance?

Prayer: God, we don't believe you have forgotten us or are hiding. Your actions may be a mystery to us, but we believe your promise never to abandon us. Give us courage and wisdom to overcome anger with love, and evil with good. Amen.

SATURDAY

Amazing Grace

SCRIPTURE READING • LUKE 23:42-43

Grace is the unmerited, undeserved, and unearned love of God showered on our lives. God offers us such love not because we are good or great—we are neither—but simply because God is love. But God's grace often surprises, and what surprises us most about God's grace related to Advent is that God would take on flesh and dwell among us.

Advent stands out as the supreme example of God's persistent grace. The whole Bible is a commentary on this persistent grace that seeks to save. Why didn't God deem Israel as hopeless because of its constant bickering, disobedience, and failure? Why wasn't Jacob cast aside because of his mischievous ways? Why wasn't David disowned for his dark, scheming, sinful behavior? Why wasn't Peter left to sink after he doubted, or cast aside after his denial of Christ? Why wasn't Saul of Tarsus, persecutor of the church, rejected as a hopeless cause?

For that matter, why has God not given up on us? We have spurned God's love, polluted God's creation, and mocked God's purposes with cruel acts of violence and rebellion. The answer is that nothing in heaven or on earth is as dogged, determined, stubborn, and persistent as the grace of God that wills to save us.

Bill Moyers produced a documentary for PBS about the hymn "Amazing Grace." He closed the documentary with an interview of the opera star Jessye

Norman, who shared how she had been invited to participate as the closing act in a concert at Wembley Stadium in London to celebrate the end of apartheid in South Africa. She chose "Amazing Grace" as her tribute to the changes that had taken place.

For twelve hours rock groups like Guns and Roses blasted the crowd through banks of speakers, riling up the fans, many of whom were already high on booze and drugs. Finally came the time for Jessye to sing. A single circle of light followed this majestic African American woman, wearing a flowing dashiki, as she strolled on stage. There was no backup band, no musical instruments, just Jessye.

The crowd became restless. Few people recognized Jessye. A voice yelled out from the crowd, calling for more Guns and Roses. Others began to take up the cry, and the situation started getting ugly. Then Jessye began to sing, unaccompanied, slowly and softly.

> Amazing grace! How sweet the sound
> that saved a wretch like me!
> I once was lost, but now am found;
> was blind, but now I see.

Jessye recounted a remarkable occurrence in Wembley Stadium that night. Seventy thousand raucous fans fell silent before her aria of grace. By the time she reached the second verse, she had the crowd in the palm of her hand. When Jessye started to sing the third verse, several thousand fans were singing along with her, searching their memories for the words they had heard long ago:

> When we've been there ten thousand years,
> bright shining as the sun,
> we've no less days to sing God's praise
> than when we'd first begun.
>
> (UMH 378)

Quietly, silently, miraculously, seventy thousand fans left the stadium. Following the concert, Jessye Norman said she had no idea what power descended on Wembley Stadium that night but attributed it to the hymn's powerful words of hope and promise. Philip Yancey, when writing about this event, commented that, "The world is thirsty for grace. When grace descends the world falls silent before it."[5] The grace of God provides the most compelling needs of our lives—forgiveness and acceptance.

The notion that God's love comes to us free of charge, with no strings attached, goes against every human instinct. It seems unrealistic or too good to be true, a concept more caught than taught. And yet Jesus (and thus Christianity) dares to claim that God's love for us is unconditional.

As his last act on the cross, Jesus forgave a convicted criminal nailed to a cross next to him. Jesus began his ministry by declaring good news to the poor (Luke 4:18), and he ended it by pardoning and assuring a dying criminal. We are reminded of Mary's affirmation, "[God has] lifted up the lowly" (Luke 1:52). The condemned man cried out, "Remember me when you come into your kingdom" (Luke 23:42). These words may only have been the cry of a desperate man. Yet Jesus replied, "Today you will be with me in Paradise" (v. 43). Jesus' words provide another shocking reminder that grace does not depend on what we have done for God but on what God has done for us.

Singing Mary's Song reminds us that grace is amazing, unearned, undeserved, unmerited, and freely given.

1. Where did Jesus, God-With-Us, come to you today?
2. What challenges or barriers—emotional, spiritual, practical—prevented you from experiencing Advent today?

Prayer: Thank you, God, for your grace. On our own, we feel frustrated and helpless. But your grace and your acceptance of us in our most despairing moments bring to us both transformation and hope. Thank you for a love that will not let us go. Amen.

WRITING YOUR MAGNIFICAT

During Advent, take time to write your own Magnificat. This week write the second verse. Use these questions to guide your work.

- What is true of God from generation to generation?
- What attributes or characteristics of God have been revealed to you?

WEEK 3: COMING OUT OF EGYPT

MARY SINGS

*"[The Mighty One] has brought down the powerful from their thrones,
and lifted up the lowly."*

LUKE 1:52

THEME

Coming out of bondage.

SUNDAY

Deliverance from Slavery

SCRIPTURE READING • MATTHEW 2:7-23

He [God] has helped his servant Israel, in remembrance of his mercy, according to the promise he made to our ancestors, to Abraham and to his descendants forever" (Luke 1:54-55). God's promise to Abram, "in you all the families of the earth shall be blessed" (Gen. 12:3), culminated in Mary's Annunciation. Mary becomes the first person to declare to the world that the Messiah is to be born and that "from now on all generations will call me blessed" (Luke 1:48). But the similarities do not end there.

Only Matthew records the incident of Joseph and Mary fleeing with their infant son to Egypt. While Moses and the Israelites escaped *from* Egypt, where the Pharaoh had decreed that the Israelite male children be killed, Jesus and his family escaped *to* Egypt to escape Herod's decree that the male children of Bethlehem be killed. The place of doom and death for Moses has become a place of refuge for Jesus. Just as Moses led the children of Israel out of bondage and into freedom, so Jesus brings deliverance and redemption to all, "for he will save his people from their sins" (Matt. 1:21). Moses' literal delivery of the Israelites from bondage prefigured the eternal deliverance from slavery to sin made possible by the birth and ministry of Jesus.

Many of us have known our own Egypt, for we have known some form of bondage. For some people bondage takes the form of alcohol or drug addiction, the nagging memory of a foolish act long past, or the effects of an abusive situation that won't release its hold. For others, it is despair and depression that gradually darken the horizons of life until everything appears gloomy. For others bondage may simply constitute being trapped by the circumstances of modern life, a form of oppression or imprisonment resulting from political circumstances, economic hardships, poor housing, lack of education, and limited prospects for earning a living wage.

I am fortunate to attend a remarkable group in my church called Celebrate Recovery. Celebrate Recovery accepts persons burdened with addiction, grief, or any kind of physical, emotional, or financial setback in their life and offers the direction of gifted and talented leadership. Nearly two hundred people gather on Friday nights for a meal followed by worship, companionship, and small group meetings. People of all ages and walks of life are drawn together by a common need—to stop the pain and hurt and to hear how God is helping others in their recovery. The time of worship is spirited, with numerous testimonies by those on the road to recovery who share the extraordinary change that has come about in their lives because of the existence of this group. An atmosphere of acceptance, warmth, and caring permeates the gatherings. Members have discovered Christ in their lives in a way they never thought possible.

This feeling of hope captures the theme of Advent—Christ has come to set the captive free. God has drawn back the curtain through these two monumental events, allowing us to see the nature and character of God. First, in the Exodus:

> "I have *observed* the misery of my people who are in Egypt; I have *heard* their cry on account of their taskmasters. Indeed, I *know* their sufferings, and I *have come* down to *deliver* them from the Egyptians, and to *bring* them up out of that land to a good

and broad land, a land flowing with milk and honey" (Exodus 3:7-8, emphasis added).

The verbs in this passage emphasize the action of God's love, reminding the Israelite slaves that God has not forgotten them. Those who were nobody, merely "dust under the chariot wheels of Pharaoh," turned out to be somebody—God's people. What Israel had experienced of God in the dark period of bondage and slavery in Egypt helped them to define who God is. Every Passover the Jews remind themselves of God's deliverance by declaring, "The LORD our God, who brought us out of the land of slavery and the house of bondage!" Israel's theology crystallized out of the pain of slavery and the exuberant joy of deliverance. What happened in the Exodus—bringing hope and freedom to those in bondage—foreshadowed what took place in the birth of Christ in Bethlehem, bringing deliverance, hope, and freedom for the entire world. God's mighty act of deliverance reached its culmination in the sending of God's son.

Mary was a refugee and lived through the pain and misery it entailed. But her trust in God carried her through. In our state of hopelessness and despair, we can affirm that Christ's presence can bring radical change. Our theology arises out of a story of redemption and deliverance.

Advent allows us to focus on the coming of Christ and the biblical theme of deliverance. That is the word that many are waiting to hear.

Singing Mary's Song reminds us of God's promise to Abram: "In you all the families of the earth shall be blessed" (Gen. 12:3).

1. Where did Jesus, God-With-Us, come to you today?
2. What challenges or barriers—emotional, spiritual, practical—prevented you from experiencing Advent today?
3. Read Exodus 3:7-8. Imagine these words written to you, for you. What has God *observed* in your life? What is your *cry*? What does God *know*? How can God come to *deliver* you? What *new land* might God bring you to? Journal your answers to one or more of these questions, or rewrite these verses for yourself.
4. Pray these words of Charles Wesley's hymn over and over, listening for God's message to you.

Hasten the joyful day which shall my sins consume,
when old things shall be done away, and all things new become.

(UMH 311)

Prayer: O God of grace and power, deliver us from our shortsightedness, which hides your presence from us. Grant us a clearer vision of your truth, a greater faith in your power, and a more confident assurance of your love. Amen.

MONDAY

The Importance of Withdrawal

SCRIPTURE READING • MATTHEW 2:13-15

The angel appeared to Joseph saying, "Get up, take the child and his mother, and flee to Egypt, and remain there until I tell you; for Herod is about to search for the child, to destroy him." Once before Joseph had faced a crisis. An angel appeared to give him guidance when he had learned of Mary's pregnancy and was considering a way to avoid public disgrace. Joseph appears to have discerned from this first encounter that doing what the angel commanded was best; so without delay, he packed up the family and fled to Egypt, where they remained until they could safely return.

Mary and Joseph had reason to be frightened. In the first century, Roman political leaders and their allies could and would put to death anyone who challenged their positions of power. The holy family was fleeing a political tyrant who had the power to destroy anything and anyone, including their son. Herod, who had already had several close family members executed for suspected treason (including a wife and several sons), had heard from the wise men that a child was born "king of the Jews." He immediately considered this infant a threat to his reign.

Joseph and Mary were forced to flee as refugees to a foreign country where they could think, pray, and live in safety. The biblical text is silent about their sojourn, and we can only imagine what transpired. But we can be sure that Mary was comforted by the words of the angel's promise:

> "Do not be afraid, Mary, for you have found favor with God. And now, you will conceive in your womb and bear a son, and you will name him Jesus. He will be great, and will be called the Son of the Most High, and the Lord God will give him the throne of his ancestor David. . . . and of his kingdom there will be no end." (Luke 1:30-33).

During a sojourn in a foreign country, this promise would have given Mary courage and enabled her to wait. Joseph had his promise as well: "Flee to Egypt, and remain there until I tell you." Joseph had the assurance that there would be a time when they could return. These promises allowed Mary and Joseph to wait with courage and hope.

A long tradition, not limited to Christianity, values withdrawal. Moses was forced to withdraw as a fugitive on the run (Exod. 2:15); while in the wilderness tending the flock of his father-in-law, he encountered God in a burning bush and his life changed forever. Elijah withdrew following his triumph on Mount Carmel and encountered God in the silence (1 Kings 19). Jesus withdrew to the wilderness, where he was tempted by the devil and in that struggle discovered the nature and purpose of his ministry. Following his Damascus Road conversion, Paul withdrew so he could ascertain the meaning and purpose of the new direction his life was taking (Gal. 1:17). Each of these men shared a common experience: they learned about themselves, about God, and about the nature and purpose of their lives.

Sometimes life requires us to withdraw from the demands, clutter, and ambiguity of our day-to-day existence, a fact that has become especially relevant in recent years. The world's pain, suffering, and bloodshed come spilling into our living rooms in real time and in graphic color. We require help to sift through this overload of mental and emotional stimulation and to make sense of what it means to live in this twenty-first-century world. We need moments to withdraw and to gain not only a new realization of who we are but also a deeper realization of who God is.

Withdrawal can be invaluable. How often did you face difficult choices and wish you had spent more time before making a decision? Maybe you are wrestling with that burning question, "How can I determine the will of God for my life?" Possibly your relationship with God and others has deteriorated; prayer, worship, and scripture don't excite you anymore. If you have come to a place where the joy and spark in your life is not what it used to be, perhaps a weekend retreat would be a fitting response. That weekend of withdrawal may bring you into contact with people asking themselves the same questions and dealing with the same struggles. When a small group meets together for renewal, they do so with a promise. Jesus said "Where two or three are gathered in my name, I am there among them" (Matt. 18:20).

Singing Mary's Song helps us to keep the promise alive.

1. Where did Jesus, God-With-Us, come to you today?
2. What challenges or barriers—emotional, spiritual, practical—prevented you from experiencing Advent today?
3. When was the last time that you withdrew—on retreat or on vacation? What gifts did you find there?
4. Make a list of the details and logistics that have to be arranged in order for you to withdraw again. Formulate a plan to act on these details. Choose a date, a place, and a person who may want to join you. Go to meet God there.

Prayer: Lord, when withdrawal brings us a deeper understanding of ourselves and you, give us the courage to face the changes in our lives that our vision of you may entail. Amen.

TUESDAY

Withdrawal Enables Return

SCRIPTURE READING • MATTHEW 2:20-23

Mary and Joseph were living in Egypt, trying to gather up the fragments of their lives and place them into a meaningful pattern. They had grown up with the hope and expectation of a coming messiah, as proclaimed by the prophets. We can imagine them trying to grasp the overwhelming reality that Mary's child *was* the promised Messiah and to determine the role they are to play.

Centuries of conjecture had given rise to numerous theories about the nature of the promised messiah. Some Jews apparently anticipated the return of King David or someone from the Davidic line. Many people assumed the Messiah would come from a prominent location—a place of power and influence. During the Roman occupation a strong desire grew for a warrior king who would bring political freedom; for some Jewish sects the expectation of a messiah who would annihilate the host of wickedness reached a fever pitch. Some groups longed so desperately for a messiah that they would accept anyone appearing on the scene who dramatically declared himself the anointed one. In most cases their hopes were dashed (often by the Roman military) as the supposed messiah would be defeated, and the movement would collapse.

In the end, common expectations of the Messiah did not fit God's plans. Instead Jesus was born amid the ordinary people in the Judean hills, in a stable among the animals rather than among the world's elite. His mother was suspected of having an affair, probably giving rise to rumors that Joseph was not his biological father. Both parents hailed from a working-class community, neither was a religious leader.

After what may have been a year or two of withdrawal in Egypt (no one knows for sure), an angel spoke to Joseph in a dream saying, "Get up, take the child and his mother, and go to the land of Israel, for those who were seeking the child's life are dead." We can picture Mary and Joseph returning with a renewed feeling of promise and hope.

This event confirms an important truth: Withdrawal is not an end in itself; withdrawal happens for the purpose of return. Again, Moses learned a valuable lesson in the wilderness when he encountered God at the burning bush, and the voice in the bush ordered him to return to Egypt to persuade an uncompromising Pharaoh to free the Israelite slaves. Moses' meeting on Mount Sinai occurred for the sole purpose of enabling him to accomplish a larger task. Likewise, God sent Elijah forth with a renewed mission. Jesus was led by the Spirit into the wilderness, where the temptations clarified the nature of his ministry. He would return from the wilderness to preach and heal.

The point of withdrawal and return lies not in seeking God somewhere else and bringing God back into the here and now. Rather, this process engages us in the exciting discovery that the God we thought was only "out there" is already "in here." Only our dimness of vision kept us from an awareness of God's presence. I don't believe that Mary and Joseph were fleeing to Egypt in search of God during their time of trial. They were aware of God's presence both before and during their stay in Egypt. The withdrawal brought them a sense of encouragement that provided assurance as they headed for Nazareth and the challenging years ahead.

We don't discover God. God has already discovered us. Our dimness of vision and our sin blind us to God's presence. Remember, the word for Advent is *Immanuel*! God is with us!

Singing Mary's Song reminds us that through the Holy Spirit, Christ has become a living presence in our midst and brings deliverance, freedom, and hope.

1. Where did Jesus, God-With-Us, come to you today?
2. What challenges or barriers—emotional, spiritual, practical—prevented you from experiencing Advent today?
3. "Withdrawal is not an end in itself. Withdrawal happens for the purpose of return." In which place are you now living—in the world, in the wilderness or in the time of preparation for return? What do you learn from the return of Joseph and Mary, Moses, Elijah, or Jesus?
4. Where do you need to see God revealed in the here and now?

Prayer: Lord, help us to see you more clearly and love you more dearly. Amen.

WEDNESDAY

Seeking Understanding

SCRIPTURE READING • LUKE 2:41-52

Withdrawal can be inspiring and the return necessary. Together, withdrawal and return provide us with fresh perspectives. The time had come for Joseph and his family to return, because Herod had died, the threat was gone, and in Nazareth Jesus could grow "in wisdom and stature" (Luke 2:52, KJV). As Jesus grew to adulthood, he waited patiently for the voice in the wilderness to declare, "Repent, for the kingdom of heaven has come near" (Matt. 3:2), indicating that his time had come. In the meantime (for the next thirty years), life would remain somewhat domestic.

Nazareth was the right place for Joseph and Mary and their family for many reasons. But one reason seems to stand out above the others—Nazareth offered community. Mark identified Nazareth as Jesus' "hometown" and listed Jesus' family members more fully than any other place in the New Testament: "Is not this the carpenter, the son of Mary and brother of James and Joses and Judas and Simon, and are not his sisters here with us?" (see Mark 6:1-3). It stands to reason that, with all of these brothers and sisters, Jesus had brothers-in-law and sisters-in-law and nieces and nephews. Imagine Mary not only basking in the midst of this extended family but also wondering when the promises regarding her oldest son would be fulfilled. We forget that God does have a timetable. Abraham was seventy-five when God promised him an heir but one hundred when Isaac was born.

One lone incident interrupts the silence of these years in Nazareth. The twelve-year-old Jesus traveled with his parents to Jerusalem for the Passover celebration. When the festival was over, his parents started the journey home, unaware that Jesus had stayed behind. As part of a large crowd of friends and family, they assumed that their son was off with friends of his own. After a day's journey, they determined that Jesus was not with them. Unable to locate him, they returned to Jerusalem, where they searched for three days before they found him in the Temple conversing with the teachers, who were amazed at this young man's knowledge.

> His mother said to him, "Child, why have you treated us like this? Look, your father and I have been searching for you in great anxiety." He said to them, "Why were you searching for me? Did you not know that I must be in my Father's house?" But they did not understand what he said to them.

These are the first words of Jesus recorded in the Gospels.

Note the tender and touching nature of the dialogue between Jesus and his mother. Mary said, "Your father and I." She called Joseph "father." But Jesus determinedly applied the word to God: "I must be in my Father's house." By making this declaration, Jesus openly set forth his identity as the Son of God and indicated that his life would be formed by his unique relationship with the Father. Luke, however, records that Mary and Joseph did not comprehend. Although Jesus knew who he was, he returned home with his parents and "was obedient to them."

Clearly the events of Jesus' birth had not prepared his parents for the nature of their son's life; they remained mystified. But the text notes in several places, "Mary treasured all these words and pondered them in her heart" (Luke 2:19; see v. 51). Alan Culpepper points out, "Treasuring experiences that are infused with God's presence can bring insight later and provide a firm foundation for a life of obedient discipleship."[1] The treasures Mary had gathered through the years brought a love and loyalty that never wavered, which led her to the foot of the cross as the disciples fled. And although Mary was not among the women who visited Jesus' tomb on the first Easter morning, she reappeared as a member of the group of believers gathered in Jerusalem on the Day of Pentecost (Acts 1:14). Mary had withdrawn in her grief but now had joined those celebrating Jesus' resurrection. In light of the Resurrection, the veil lifted and she could now appreciate the divine purpose of Jesus' life, death, and resurrection.

Mary prevailed because she saw a new day coming. She spoke her hope into existence—the Lord had looked with favor on the lowliness of God's servant and God had "done great things for her." She believed, even when it appeared there was nothing to believe in.

Two thousand years later, how is it with you? Do you find the story hard to believe? Or do you still believe a new day is coming? Do you question that Jesus is who he says he is—Savior, Redeemer, and Lord? Or do you still believe that God is creator and sustainer of the heavens and the earth, whose love proves so great that we are never out of bounds? This is the hope of Advent—to discover who Jesus Christ is, making him the center of our lives, bringing us to a new day.

Singing Mary's Song reminds us that God's delays are not denials.

1. Where did Jesus, God-With-Us, come to you today?
2. What challenges or barriers—emotional, spiritual, practical—prevented you from experiencing Advent today?
3. Choose one of the questions in the last paragraph of the meditation and make a list of your questions, doubts, concerns, and hopes. Spend time in conversation with God today, using this list as your guide.
4. Mary's story reminds us that God's delays are not our denials. What denial in your life requires transforming? Does it help you to think of it as a delay? What hope or fresh vision does this new perspective give you?

Prayer: Gracious God, in our Advent journey may our hearts be so open to you that no corner of our lives will be unillumined by the light of your presence. Let there be nothing within us to darken that light. Amen.

THURSDAY
A New Message
SCRIPTURE READING • JOHN 2:1-12

John the Baptist lived in the desert and presented an unkempt appearance (with a shirt of camel's hair and a diet of locusts and wild honey) but was nonetheless effective. The people from Jerusalem, Judea, and the region around the Jordan flocked to hear him preach "and were baptized by him in the river Jordan, confessing their sins" (Mark 1:5). John preached a message of repentance and terror, of urgency, of divine judgment about to fall. But John's message centered on the coming messiah and eventually gave way to Jesus' message of newness and reconciliation. John realized and accepted the inevitable outcome: as Jesus' influence increased, his own would decrease (John 3:30).

Mary appears to have learned a similar lesson. Jesus, fully grown and having begun his public ministry, attended a wedding in Cana of Galilee; his mother and his disciples were there as well. To the horror of the bride and her family, the wine, an essential element to the feast, ran out. Instinctively, Mary turned to Jesus: "They have no wine."

Jesus responded, "Woman, what concern is that to you and to me?" The term *woman* sounds harsh and apparently distances Jesus from his mother and from the problem at hand.

Mary does not specifically tell Jesus what to do but turns to the servants and says in a commanding voice, "Do whatever he tells you."

This story represents perhaps the most difficult New Testament depiction of Mary. Some see in the dialogue a person who did not understand Jesus' purposes. Others suggest this episode illustrates a necessary distancing that must come about in the relationship between mother and son now that Jesus' public ministry had begun. Regardless, the story makes clear that Mary believed in Jesus even when she did not fully comprehend what he was doing and even when he had refused her request to help. But in this instance she seemed willing to relinquish the perception of the son she had known and to accept who he had become. So she tells others, "Listen to him. He will do the right thing." Like John the Baptist, Mary has understood that her knowledge of Jesus must "increase." Mary too had grown in wisdom and understanding during those many years of caring for her son in Nazareth.

We desire to grow in the newness of faith, commitment, stewardship, and servitude for peace and justice. But within this desire lie old, habitual, and destructive factors that must decrease in order that the new life-giving power of Christ may increase and grow in us.

Walter Brueggemann instructs us to

- Decrease what is greedy, what is frantic consumerism, for the increase of simple, life-giving sharing.

- Decrease what is fearful and defensive, for the increase of life-giving compassion and generosity.
- Decrease what is fraudulent and pretense, for the increase of life-giving truth telling in your life, truth telling about you and your neighbor, about the sickness of our society and our enmeshment in that sickness.
- Decrease what is hateful and alienating, for the increase of healing and forgiveness, which finally are the only source of life.[2]

Advent is the time for discovery. Our discovery can lead to promises that create a dawning of new life and living. Advent is a time for the old—that which has lost its meaning, purpose, and enthusiasm—to "decrease." Advent provides a time to develop a new awareness of Christ that brings inspiration, adventure, freedom, and hope. Such is the newness of the gospel! The new insight that we gain during Advent about the love, grace, mercy, hope, forgiveness, and new life in Christ means little unless we commit every aspect of our lives to that truth. Otherwise we fail to develop in our Christian life, and we risk becoming complacent and falling short of the demands that being followers of God place on us.

Singing Mary's Song reminds us that we are called to give witness to the One who scattered the proud, brought down rulers, and lifted up the poor.

1. Where did Jesus, God-With-Us, come to you today?
2. What challenges or barriers—emotional, spiritual, practical—prevented you from experiencing Advent today?
3. Reread Walter Brueggemann's list of "decreases." Which one sounds the most difficult for you? Which one feels most relevant to your life now?
4. "New life in Christ means little unless we commit every aspect of our lives to that truth." Do you believe this statement? Why or why not? If yes, do you believe it enough to commit to a new plan of action this Advent?

Prayer: God of abundance, help us to take mystery, disappointment, suspense, and danger and use them to gain assurance, patience, perseverance, and courage. Create in us, O Lord, clean hearts and right spirits. Amen.

FRIDAY

Recovering Wonder

SCRIPTURE READING • LUKE 2:41-42

We earlier discussed Luke's emphasis on Mary and Joseph's being loyal Jewish parents who conscientiously fulfilled the requirements of the law. They had Jesus circumcised when he was eight days old and went to the Temple for Mary's act of purification. They traveled to Jerusalem every year for the Feast of the Passover, and when Jesus came of age they saw to it that he accompanied them. They lived as part of a covenant community and ensured that Jesus was also a part of this community.

Humans often fall into the temptation that allows religious observances to transform into ends in themselves and not celebrations of what God has accomplished. When religious life becomes merely obeying laws and keeping observances, people lose sight of the law's main focus—love for God and neighbor. Jesus faced this problem when he confronted the hypocrisy of the religious leaders of his day. When religious practice degenerates into meaningless ceremonies, it no longer relates to the trials of contemporary life and calcifies. A vibrant faith relates to the world here and now.

The image of Mary and Joseph presenting their son in the Temple challenges us to recover the sense of wonder and mystery of God's presence in everyday encounters through ritual celebration and daily life. In our modern world, pressures from secularism and the pace of life have reduced the practice of many meaningful rituals. Many families no longer take time to pray before meals or to practice serious reflection as a daily family activity because they no longer eat meals as families anymore—the dinner table has been replaced by TV trays. For far too many people, religious rituals have been reduced to Christmas and Easter services and to attendance at baptisms, weddings, and funerals. Our fast pace of life, emphasis on secular interests, and the distraction of technology jeopardize the possibility that we may recognize the holy in the ordinariness of daily activity.

One day a woman entered my office and exclaimed, "God just answered my prayer!" She had arrived at the doctor's office and found the parking lot full. She was not feeling well and sought a parking place near the office. She prayed she circled the lot, telling God how desperately she needed the parking place, and then, "Behold, God opened a place for me right in front of the office!"

On the one hand, I tend to downplay the notion that God, with the numerous cares of the world—war, death, natural disasters, the homeless and hungry—would take time to find this woman a parking place. But I realized that in doing so I risked missing an important lesson. I had nearly failed to recognize how this parishioner looked for and sensed the presence of God in the most common of everyday occurrences.

Rituals are not restrictive. Liturgy evokes power because words contain power. When Mary and Joseph presented their son at the Temple, they celebrated the mystery and the goodness of life in the Jewish community. The Eucharist gives love a voice. Baptism puts forth a promise of shared relationships among parents, congregations, and God.

Christmas Eve services have grown in popularity, and in some churches more people attend worship on Christmas Eve than on Easter. Since Christmas is a time for families to gather, many attend Christmas Eve services as a group. Many of these services blend a celebration of the Eucharist and traditional Christmas music with the high energy of contemporary worship. When we celebrate Communion, we participate as a part of the covenant community, expressing sacramental love. We receive the promise: "Hear the good news: Christ died for us while we were yet sinners; that proves God's love for us. In the name of Jesus Christ you are forgiven! Glory to God. Amen" (UMBW 35).

Christmas Communion reminds us that "we are like the children of Israel in the wilderness, tasting the fruit plucked from the promised land. It is the future coming to meet us in the present."[3] For Christ has died; Christ is risen; Christ will come again.

Singing Mary's Song reminds us we are called to seek out those times in everyday life when we can exclaim, "My soul magnifies the Lord, and my spirit rejoices in God my Savior!"

1. Where did Jesus, God-With-Us, come to you today?
2. What challenges or barriers—emotional, spiritual, practical—prevented you from experiencing Advent today?

3. What are your family rituals? How can you invite God into the midst of these rituals?

4. Imagine the Advent story in a world of cell phones, Internet, and text messages. How can we recover the intimacy of a family traveling together, earthy shepherds kneeling in the stable, the beauty of a bright star?

5. Pray for those in your covenant community, the group (large or small) that celebrates with you, prays with you, and loves you unconditionally.

Prayer: Lord, as we leave your table, grant that we may go into the world in the strength of your Spirit to give ourselves for others. Amen.

SATURDAY

All about Love

SCRIPTURE READING • 1 JOHN 3:18

During the years that Mary raised her son and contemplated what he would become, we can envision her longing for the day when God's justice (as she eloquently expressed it in the Magnificat) would become a reality and living out that faith in her own life. At some level, she must have grasped the truth later expressed in one of John's letters, "We love because [God] first loved us" (1 John 4:19). The "new thing" coming to pass through the life of her son would involve God's love.

How can we express to this world of violence, war, hunger, homelessness, and pain that the God who comes among us in the birth of Jesus is a God "full of grace and truth"? Walter Wink notes the following:

> As the Crucified, Jesus thus identifies with every victim of tor-
> ture, incest, or rape; with every peasant caught in the cross fire
> of enemy patrols; with each of the forty thousand children who
> die each day from starvation. . . . with every Alzheimer's patient

slowly losing the capacity of recognition. . . . In Jesus we see the suffering of God with and in suffering people."[4]

One of the worst kinds of suffering is to feel that no one cares. Given the amount of pain, disappointment, sorrow, and grief that burdens the hearts of many amid the masses living on the dark side of life, where the sun never seems to shine, this could be the Advent when Christ's love, comfort, and healing break through and "the mournful, broken hearts rejoice, the humble poor believe."

The difference that the birth of Jesus Christ made for this world can be summed up in the phrase "God's love became incarnate." Jesus' life defines it. The love incarnate in Jesus knew life exactly as we know it—every pain, every tear, every aspect. Walter Brueggemann recounted a story about a colleague dying from cancer who, as he was dying reached up, grabbed Brueggemann's hand, and said, "Walter, it's all about love."

When we think about the love of God radiating through human flesh and blood, our thoughts may turn to Saint Francis of Assisi, Mother Teresa, Dorothy Day, or Dietrich Bonhoeffer—characters who have inspired us for years. But what about those quiet saints who walk our streets and live with the same struggles and strains of life that we do, yet cast a radiance of love, caring, self-giving, and hope that we wish we had? Through it all, they possess a keen feeling of purpose, confidence, and assurance. They know who they are and they know where they are going.

Richard Smith was a quiet saint. He earned his law degree and served as an officer in World War II, the Korean War, and the war in Vietnam. He was an active, lifelong member of the church and served on several conference boards. But he also spoke prophetic words of concern when it came to issues of peace with justice and other social concerns on both a local and national level. Though soft-spoken and unassuming, when something needed saying, he would say it in his own quiet, persuasive way.

Richard's principles, values, moral convictions, and character reflected his deep love for Christ and his church. His moral convictions and a deep desire for honesty and fair play drove him to defend those less fortunate who had no one else to stand up for them, especially in a court of law. Richard's *pro bono* work schedule was amazing. Every Monday for over twenty years he volunteered at a legal aid clinic, helping to draft wills, contracts, powers of attorney, or just to serve as a friend to those less fortunate. On numerous occasions he bought clothing for his clients so they would look good in court. The day before his death Richard worked at the clinic. During those same years he provided legal service at another nearby center. He and his wife advocated for peace with women's rights, social equality, and education.

During the years that I served as Richard's pastor, he encouraged me with letters of support and offered helpful, honest criticism. I have learned that when certain people (including Richard) offer a critical response, I should listen. His sense of Christ's grace and compassion in his life enabled him to express that compassion and grace to others. The issues of his faith were the issues of his life.

When he died, I had the privilege of conducting Richard's service of celebration. I closed with these words from the liturgy: "Merciful savior, accept Richard into the arms of your mercy, into the blessed rest of everlasting peace, into the glorious company of the saints of light" (UMBW 150).

The quiet saint dwells with the community of saints. It is all about love!

Singing Mary's Song reminds us that the call of Christ in our lives is to seek justice with love.

1. Where did Jesus, God-With-Us, come to you today?
2. What challenges or barriers—emotional, spiritual, practical—prevented you from experiencing Advent today?

Prayer: Thank-you, O God, for those humble servants who have dedicated their lives to be Christ's servants in service to others. Help us to discover the joy that such service can bring. May this be the Advent that we hear the call of Christ to a new level of discipleship. Amen.

WRITING YOUR MAGNIFICAT

During Advent, take time to write your own Magnificat. This week write the third verse. Use these questions to guide your work.

- What difference does the birth of Jesus make for this world?
- What circumstances can be different? How?

WEEK 4: PREPARING FOR JESUS' BIRTH

MARY SINGS

"[The Lord] has filled the hungry with good things,
and sent the rich away empty."

LUKE 1:53

THEME

The birth of Christ fills us with a sense of wonder and expectation.

SUNDAY

Good news for all people

SCRIPTURE READING • MATTHEW 1:18-25; LUKE 2:8-20; JOHN 1:1-18

When the angels announced Jesus' birth, they chose from among all the people on earth to speak to the shepherds. These shepherds were not idyllic figures as we tend to envision them as rough and tough, unkempt men of the Judean hill country. They were part of the "migrant workers" of first-century Palestine; were prevented from observing many of the ceremonial laws, since they cared for the sheep twenty-four hours a day; and were thus shunned by the orthodox religious people of society. Shepherds were considered unclean, unfit to enter the Temple, synagogues, and probably polite company.

Imagine the shepherds huddled together for warmth on the hillside that night when an angelic host announced to them: "I am bringing you good news of great joy for all the people: to you is born this day in the city of David a Savior, who is the Messiah, the Lord" (Luke 2:10-11).

This pronouncement fits perfectly with Mary's claims that God will scatter the proud, bring down the powerful, and lift up the lowly (see Luke 1:51-52). The story of the shepherds follows Luke's theology that Jesus' birth revealed a new world order, a world no longer under the power of Caesar but under the direction of God. God desires the redemption of everyone, everywhere, even in the most remote and dire circumstances. The shepherds qualify for Luke's guest list for the kingdom of God: the poor, the crippled, the blind, and the lame (see Luke 14:21). They belong in the story because they help to relate Jesus to the shepherd king David (2 Sam. 7:8).

We see again the theme that the God of creation has come to Bethlehem amid the mire and poverty of a stable in a village where the streets were crowded, where angry voices spouted profanity, and where life remained cheap. And yet, in this unlikely setting, Mary gave birth to a Son who gives glory to God in the highest among the lowest and brings new hope and a new day for the world. No wonder the angel shouted out that night to those shepherds huddled on the hillside, "I am bringing you good news of great joy for all the people."

Listen again to the familiar story of Bethlehem. Do not allow its familiarity to deaden your feeling of wonder. Dag Hammarskjöld said, "God does not die on the day when we cease to believe in a personal deity, but we die on the day when our lives cease to be illumined by the steady radiance, renewed daily, of a wonder, the source of which is beyond all reason."[1] The instant we cease to believe that God exists, wonder leaves our lives. We have been bombarded with cable news and become so addicted to information that we find ourselves numb to feeling and mystery. Advent should be a time when we walk on tiptoe with hushed voices, because we feel that something great is about to happen. We share Isaiah's longing, which caused him to cry out to God, "O that you would tear open the heavens and come down" (64:1). That longing injects wonder into our bloodstream and mystery and expectation as well.

Again this year, the Advent story will be read in nearly every part of the world, in numerous dialects and languages; dramatized in pageants, cantatas, concerts; and the message proclaimed through sermons and homilies from the cathedrals of Europe to the thatched-roof churches in remote villages of Africa, to the thousands of house churches scattered throughout China. The story of Advent projects a message that has the power to bring change, hope, and transformation to every human life that will listen, accept, and believe. Some people will consider it interesting, amusing, or entertaining—merely a fantasy like *The Lion King* or *The Swan Princess*. For others, the message of the story of Advent will be too good to be true.

Unfortunately, the story of Advent has become so wrapped in sentimental embroidery that its stark realism may be lost. Its characters have acquired celebrity status, becoming something quite out of this world. But the characters of Advent were not people with halos but ordinary men and women with their own fears and frustrations and anxieties and hopes, just like us. The shepherds were ordinary people facing ordinary lives, looked down upon by many and struggling to make ends meet. Mary and Joseph were ordinary people as well, who knew the stress and strain of a struggling family business and the emotional struggle of raising children (the oldest whom they often misunderstood). But they were chosen by God to play a role in this drama, and we can surmise that they were people of humble faith with a sincere commitment to do the will of God. Within this collection of working-class people, in the Judean hill country, we come face-to-face with God.

According to Luke, God did not reveal God's vision for the world through the powerful or socially elite but through a humble handmaiden of the Lord. Mary will continue to sing her song; the world will continue to listen; and many will believe. And the results will prove to be revolutionary.

Singing Mary's Song reminds us that the Mighty One has done great things for us. Holy is the name of the Lord.

1. Where did Jesus, God-With-Us, come to you today?
2. What challenges or barriers—emotional, spiritual, practical—prevented you from experiencing Advent today?
3. Where do you see wonder in your world? How can you recover the awe and mystery and beauty of the Advent story?
4. Imagine telling the story of Jesus' birth to someone outside the church. What strikes you as amazing, fantastical, or wondrous?
5. Consider people you know. Who needs to have this wonder and hope injected into their lives? How can you participate?

Prayer: Wondrous God, this Advent lead us to seek new discoveries and to go where we have never gone before. Help us, O Lord, to allow for the singing of angels. Amen.

MONDAY

Those Who Believed in His Name
SCRIPTURE READING • JOHN 1:12

Mark opens his Gospel with the words, "The beginning of the good news of Jesus Christ, the Son of God" (1:1). Likewise, Zechariah declared it as good news: "By the tender mercy of our God, the dawn from on high will break upon us, to give light to those who sit in darkness and in the shadow of death, to guide our feet into the way of peace" (Luke 1:78-79). So did Simeon: "Master, now you are dismissing your servant in peace" (2:29). And of course, Mary: "[The Lord's] mercy is for those who fear him from generation to generation" (1:50). But this good news for some served as bad news for others. The news of Jesus' birth sounds good for those who suffer pain but bad for those who inflict pain, good for the hungry but bad for those who cause hunger, and good for the oppressed but bad for those who cause oppression.

The coming of Christ served as good news in the life of Shirley and her husband, Bob. They were a remarkably gifted, talented, and loving couple. Both were linguists (Shirley spoke seven languages) who met in graduate school, fell in love, married, and left soon after to become Wycliffe Bible translators in the wilds of New Guinea. There they would raise their children and spend the next forty years. After working for several years with the people of their village, Bob and Shirley had learned the language, developed a written script for it, and completed a translation of the New Testament for the indigenous people.

In 1994, Shirley was diagnosed with Alzheimer's disease, which slowly took its toll. She struggled but finally had to give up her work and return to Florida. Bob found a few acres outside of Tallahassee, heavily forested and the bearing the closest resemblance to New Guinea. Bob devoted his entire life to caring for Shirley. One day when I was visiting, Shirley, who was sitting next to Bob, developed a frightening stare and stiffened. Bob reached out and pulled her close, placing her head on his shoulder. She closed her eyes—calm, peaceful, and secure in Bob's embrace.

Alzheimer's had taken away Shirley's extraordinary gifts and talents, her recognition of others, and her speech. It had taken away her world and would finally take her life. But it could not take away her life's accomplishments. The translation of the New Testament illustrates her commitment to the people she loved. It will continue to bring inspiration, hope, and new life in Christ to many by sharing the good news of Christ's coming. Her life will continue to cast a long shadow of influence for many years to come.

There are those for whom the coming of Christ was a time of rejection and disbelief; but to those "who received him, who believed in his name, he gave power to become children of God" (John 1:12).

Singing Mary's Song reminds us that God looks with favor on those servants who labor in the lowest and the darkest corners of this world.

1. Where did Jesus, God-With-Us, come to you today?
2. What challenges or barriers—emotional, spiritual, practical—prevented you from experiencing Advent today?
3. When have you experienced good news and bad news as two sides of the same coin? a move? a new job? a marriage or divorce? Journal about the conflicting perspectives and emotions.
4. What do you discern from Shirley's story and other saints who live and die for the Lord in each circumstance?

Prayer: Gracious God, we are grateful for those who dare to believe in the incredible story of Jesus' birth and, in believing, have become your children, proclaiming the message of reconciliation, hope, love, and peace with justice throughout the world. O Lord, may the light of Bethlehem's love and hope continue to shine. Amen.

TUESDAY
The Cost of Discipleship
SCRIPTURE READING • JOHN 1:9-11

Although the Gospel of John does not record the story of Jesus' birth, the words of John's Prologue (1:1-18) provide a theological description of the accounts of his birth as recorded in Matthew and Luke. The Prologue refers to Christ's preexistence—"In the beginning was the Word, and the Word was with God" (1:1)—and captures the essence of the birth narrative in one verse—"And the Word became flesh and lived among us . . . full of grace and truth" (1:14). New Testament scholars have suggested that John wrote his entire Gospel as an exposition on this one verse. The Greek verb translated "lived" actually means "pitched his tent," recalling God's dwelling with Israel in the desert following their escape from slavery in Egypt. The Word becoming flesh proved a decisive turning point in human history, when God's relationship to humanity changed dramatically. God becoming flesh served not only as a turning point but also as a dramatic moment when humanity could henceforth see, know, and experience God in ways never before possible.

The role Mary plays in the Gospel of John differs greatly from her roles in Matthew, Luke, and (her brief mention in) Mark (6:3). John never mentions Mary by name: she appears at the wedding at Cana as "the mother of Jesus" (chapter 2) and again at the foot of the cross as "his mother" (19:25-26); in another instance, the Jews ask "is this not Jesus, the son of Joseph, whose father and mother we know?" (6:42). For John, Mary's significance stems less from her part at the manger than from her presence at the cross.

When Jesus looked down from the cross and saw his mother, many thoughts must have crossed his mind. At times she had not understood his behavior, but she alone had accompanied him from birth until death. She had nurtured him in his youth and been with him through the death of his father. As Mary looked up at her son's broken body streaked with blood, she must have thought about the night of his birth when his body was streaked with her blood. We can imagine her, trembling and overwhelmed by emotion, remembering the words of the angel, "Greetings, favored one! The Lord is with you" (Luke 1:28), and the promise that she would bear a son who would be great and whose kingdom would never end. Now Mary was experiencing firsthand the "scandal of the cross." This was not the end she would have envisioned!

One of my favorite retreat sites displays a large white cross on a high bluff overlooking a lake. When I first visited the area, a colleague informed me it was a pleasant three-mile run around the lake. I saw my friend the next day after finishing my run and told him that I had enjoyed it right up until the end, when I encountered a steep incline leading up to the cross at the top of the hill. He explained to me that I had gone the wrong way. "Stay on the footpath around the cross. It's much easier."

Many people find the Cross, with its message of strength through defeat, difficult and offensive. The temptation arises to "go around" the Cross because that way presents a path that seems much easier. We much prefer a message of wealth, success, power, and prosperity. An ABC correspondent was interviewing a pastor of a large megachurch and asked him, "If you are a Christian church, why don't you have any Christian symbols, especially the cross?" His reply was, "So as not to offend anyone who comes to worship." Paul declared, "We proclaim Christ crucified, a stumbling block to the Jews and foolishness to Gentiles" (1 Cor. 1:23).

In each Gospel account, Mary stands at the cross but does not speak a word. Her role is to stand near the cross. As Mary leads us from the birth in Bethlehem to the Crucifixion at Golgotha, the Cross inevitably emerges as an aspect of our Advent reflections. Jesus' birth foreshadows (and remains meaningless without) his death.

The Cross reminds us of the great cost God paid for our salvation. It calls us to a community of mutual, self-giving love and to bear one another's burdens. True community requires the willingness to let our self-centered lives die and to be born into new life in Christ, in solidarity with each of our fellow creatures.

The apostle Paul stated it clearly by saying,

> I appeal to you therefore, brothers and sisters, by the mercies of God, to present your bodies as a living sacrifice, holy and acceptable to God, which is your spiritual worship. Do not be

conformed to this world, but be transformed by the renewing of your minds, so that you may discern what is the will of God—what is good and acceptable and perfect (Rom. 12:1-2).

The cost of discipleship has never been less!

Singing Mary's Song reminds us that discipleship comes at a cost.

1. Where did Jesus, God-With-Us, come to you today?
2. What challenges or barriers—emotional, spiritual, practical—prevented you from experiencing Advent today?
3. Stand with Mary at the foot of the cross. Imagine the pain of a mother and the confusion of a disciple. Make them your own.
4. When have you suffered the pain of vulnerability or the cost of loving someone deeply? In what ways was it worth the risk?

Prayer: Save us, O God, from those sins that so easily beset us, from lives of complacency, and from having a greater interest in our personal well-being than that of others. Help us to be the people you would have us be, and bring to us the transformation that only you can bring. Amen.

WEDNESDAY

Persistent in Faith

SCRIPTURE READING • ACTS 1:12-14

The final reference to Mary in the New Testament (Acts 1:14) places her among the many followers of Jesus who came together following his resurrection (as he had commanded at his ascension) and who joined together in constant prayer. But again, as at the cross, Mary remains silent.

We recall from Luke's birth narrative that Mary and Joseph were pious Jews. Luke records that when the shepherds shared what they angel had told them,

Mary "treasured all these words and pondered them in her heart" (2:19). Luke also records that when the twelve-year-old Jesus asked his frantic parents, "Did you not know that I must be in my Father's house?" that Mary "treasured all these things in her heart" during the time that he "increased in wisdom and in years" (2:49-52).

The word *ponder* has several meanings: "to weigh in the mind; to think about: to reflect on; to think or consider esp. quietly, soberly, and deeply."[2] Pondering suggests that Mary did not allow these memories to fade, that they provided her the opportunity to hold on to those instances and to reflect on their meaning and purpose. We might consider that as a young girl, Mary had been overwhelmed by these events—the Annunciation, the journey to Bethlehem, the birth of her son, the visitation by the shepherds, Jesus' response in the Temple—but that she relived these moments of joy and fulfillment often.

Mary's response to the angel at her Annunciation, "Here am I, the servant of the Lord; let it be with me according to your word" (Luke 1:38), encapsulates her life of faith. Mary's trust and obedient response set the stage for God's plan to bring salvation to everyone. In spite of the risk, in spite of the doubt and uncertainty that followed her to the cross and beyond, she apparently never wavered from her call. Her pondering provided clarity in her personal faith, which guided her and allowed her to remain silent when confronted by circumstances she did not understand. Mary pondered over a son profoundly hers even when he was no longer hers at all. The promises she had received gave her the strength to endure: "You will . . . bear a son . . . he will be great . . . the Lord God will give to him the throne of his ancestor David . . . and of his kingdom there will be no end" (Luke 1:31-33).

Mary accepted these promises as true and trustworthy. Her ponderings gave her the strength to endure, to overcome fear, and to work for peace.

Amid her struggles, contemplation, and reflection, Mary remained persistent in faith and arrived at that triumphant instant when—with Peter, the other disciples and the women in Jerusalem—she lived through the dawn of Pentecost. Mary remained faithful to her calling as a humble servant of God.

Doubt and uncertainty often confront us in our Christian journey. God's timing and apparent delays can seem like denials. Silence from on high may stifle our willingness to endure. Feelings of fear and rejection begin to set in.

We cannot be joyful or truly love one another if we are fearful, because fear suffocates hope.

Like the angels in the birth narratives who admonish people to "fear not!" the book of Isaiah proclaims:

> Strengthen the weak hands,
>   and make firm the feeble knees.
> Say to those who are of a fearful heart,
>   "Be strong, do not fear!
> Here is your God."
>
> —Isaiah 35:3

Advent is a new day dawning. "Fear not!" The liberating God of the Exodus is on the move again in a dramatic manner, bringing deliverance and freedom. God's coming in Jesus Christ has fundamentally changed the world. The coming of Christ into human history has brought God closer than ever before. Everything is different now. Across the centuries come the words of the prophet, "Do not fear. Here is your God!"

Phillips Brooks writes,

> Yet in thy dark streets shineth the everlasting light;
> the hopes and fears of all the years are met in thee tonight.
>
> (UMH 230)

Singing Mary's Song reminds us that the love of God in Jesus Christ casts out fear.

1. Where did Jesus, God-With-Us, come to you today?
2. What challenges or barriers—emotional, spiritual, practical—prevented you from experiencing Advent today?
3. You have been given time and space to "ponder" for nearly four weeks. How have these ponderings changed your perspective, your emotions, and your actions?
4. What do you sense in the silence—expectant waiting or toe-tapping impatience, fear, or hope?
5. Remember today that love casts out fear.

Prayer: O God, you are our refuge when we are exhausted by life's efforts, bewildered by life's problems, and wounded by life's sorrows. You are "our refuge and strength, a very present help in trouble" (Ps. 46:1). Amen.

~~

THURSDAY

A Gift to Be Shared

SCRIPTURE READING • LUKE 1:52-53

The Gospel of Luke, beginning with Mary's song, emphasizes God's special concern for the poor and calls us as Christians to share that concern. For this reason, the season of Advent evokes a divine love that we freely receive and that we can now freely give, a forgiveness that has been realized and that can now be shared, and an awareness that God has reached out to us so that we can reach out to others. We have been called by God through Jesus Christ to a higher way of life, a deeper and more meaningful sense of joy, and a renewed call to serve others living in need.

When I think about God calling us to a deeper and more meaningful sense of love and joy and sharing, I remember my friend Lenny. I met Lenny when he was eighty-one years old, only a few days after his doctor informed him that his heart disease had worsened and that he had about six months to live. Lenny came from a rural community in the Florida Panhandle where, along with his extended family, he had been a lifelong member of a small Baptist church. Whenever he reminisced, he would recall this church, where he was nurtured as a child; "gave his heart to Jesus" and was baptized at age twelve; and where, at age eighteen, he and his seventeen-year-old bride, Ellen, were married. He would say, "It's just like yesterday."

Within a few months of his marriage, the church sent Lenny off with its blessing as a soldier in World War II. He described that day, when he boarded the train and said good-bye, as the darkest moment in his life. Going off to war, he did not know whether he would ever see his young bride again. In Seattle he boarded a troopship for an unknown destination; after forty days of rough seas, the ship approached the island of Guam in the south Pacific, where the soldiers were herded into a landing craft and instructed to keep looking for the American flag on the cliffs above the beach. The sighting of the American flag would mean they had taken the beach. At that point in the retelling, Lenny would reach for my hand and say, "Brother Jack, I remember how I prayed then. I said, 'Lord, I have given my life to you. If I live or die, I am yours.' I prayed that same prayer when I learned about my diagnosis."

Ellen would stand at the foot of his bed as he reminisced, a slight, stately woman, with bright eyes surrounded by a taut, wrinkled face. She wore an apron, held a towel in her hand, and flashed a pleasant smile. As Lenny talked, she nodded to me, affirming her husband's comments.

Lenny was grateful for the full life he had lived and especially for the sixty-three years that he and Ellen had spent together. He understood that he would not get well but believed that God had previously helped him in times of difficulties in preparation for this occurrence and that God would "bring him through." The devastating diagnosis could not take away Lenny's love for God or dampen the joy of his realization of God's grace, even as he grew weaker and was confined to his bed. In a more somber tone, Lenny confided in me that the most difficult part was leaving Ellen.

Lenny and Ellen lived a meager existence. Their house and its furnishings were old but neat, clean, and welcoming. Ellen always greeted me graciously at the door and poured coffee and served baked goods in a manner that made me feel at home. Whenever I asked her how things were going, she would always respond, "As good as can be expected." As Lenny's condition worsened and demanded more care, she assured me the Lord would give her the strength for her task. Similarly, Lenny would always greet me with the same words, "Brother Jack, what's the good word for today?" When I answered, "God is good," he would reply, "You've got that right."

One day Lenny disclosed a secret. Several years earlier, a member of his church had asked to borrow $15,000, most of Lenny and Ellen's life savings. The man explained that he needed the money desperately, had prayed, and that God sent him to Lenny. When Lenny mentioned what a hardship losing his savings would create for him and Ellen, the man assured him that he could be trusted to repay the loan quickly. So Lenny had given him the money. Ten years had passed and not a cent had been repaid. The loss of their savings had caused an enormous hardship for him and Ellen over the years. Although the man still attended their church, he always avoided them.

Lenny said to me, "I know that I am dying. I sent him a letter last week and told him that I forgive his debt; it is paid in full."

"Why did you do that?" I asked.

"Maybe he has a hardship I don't know about. I didn't want him to have that burden on his conscience after I am gone."

Lenny's action incorporated the true spirit of Advent, demonstrating a forgiveness that has been experienced and can now be shared. God has reached out to us and now we can reach out to others.

Singing Mary's Song reminds us that the love we have received from God is to be freely given to others.

1. Where did Jesus, God-With-Us, come to you today?
2. What challenges or barriers—emotional, spiritual, practical—prevented you from experiencing Advent today?
3. Where have you felt love in these past few weeks?
4. Where have you recognized the need for forgiveness?
5. What new awareness of God inspires you to reach out to others?

Prayer: Gracious God, you have freely given us your love, grace, and forgiveness. Grant that we may be gracious people, becoming channels of love and grace to others. Amen.

FRIDAY

The Word Continues to Become Flesh

SCRIPTURE READING • JOHN 3:16

This week many churches will light the fourth candle on the Advent wreath, the candle of Love. Typically the biblical passage read with the lighting of the fourth candle is John 3:16: "God so loved the world that he gave his only Son." For many believers, this single verse expresses the heart of the gospel message and captures the message and spirit of Mary's song. This verse represents the only place in the fourth Gospel that says God "gave," rather than "sent," his Son, emphasizing that the Incarnation derives from God's love for the world. This single verse teaches us that the origin and initiative of salvation lies solely with God, identifies the center of God's being as love, and defines the depth of God's love.[3]

The letter of First John expands our understanding of God's love: "Whoever does not love does not know God, for God is love" (4:8). "God is love, and those who abide in love abide in God" (4:16). In the Bible, these two verses alone contain the proclamation that "God is love," a sublime declaration of God's nature.

As discussed earlier, the apostle Paul wrote, "When the fullness of time had come, God sent his Son" (Gal. 4:4), an affirmation that God alone had appointed the time (the reign of Herod) and the place (Bethlehem) to break into history to bring the promised redemption. Christians affirm that God's love provided the initiative in bringing about the time and place for Jesus' birth: "For God so loved . . . he gave his only Son." Truly, God is love.

Jesus came not only at the initiative of God's love but also to help us to understand God's love for us and to place God's love at the center of our lives. God's love constitutes the center of the Christian ethic, determining our action, speech, and behavior. When this occurs, love becomes transforming.

New Testament scholar David Rensberger illustrates how the belief that love stands at the heart of the Christian life grew out of the teachings of Jesus.[4] Jesus affirmed that the two greatest commandments were these: "You shall love the Lord your God with all your heart, and with all your soul, and with all your mind, and with all your strength" (Mark 12:30; cf. Deut. 6:5), and "You shall love your neighbor as yourself" (Mark 12:31; cf. Lev. 19:18). This latter verse is quoted from a section of the Bible whose central theme is the statement, "You shall be holy, for I the LORD your God am holy" (Lev. 19:2). For Jesus, we become holy when we imitate God by performing deeds that reflect God's mercy and love to others—both our neighbors and our enemies. For the writers of the New Testament (including First John), Christians manifest God's love not only by imitating God but by imitating Christ as well. We are to walk in the light as God is in the light (1 John 1:5-7), to love one another as God loves us (4:11, 19), to walk as Jesus walked (2:6), to do what is righteous as he is righteous (3:7), to purify ourselves as he is pure (3:3), and to go so far as to lay down our lives for one another as Jesus laid down his life for us (3:16). The demand of the gospel has never been any less.

Rensberger concludes, "Christian love is the ongoing revelation of God." We share the knowledge of God's love for others through our imitation of Christ. Just as Jesus' love for us made God known, our love for one another makes God known. The love of God arrives at its intended goal when those who have received it live in love for one another. We have the opportunity every day to reveal God to the world.

How can this love be incarnate in us? We live in an age over two thousand years removed from the miracle of Bethlehem. How can we recapture and relive those moments? How are we going to get to Bethlehem? Mary and Joseph went to Bethlehem under a decree by the emperor to do so. The shepherds received dramatic instructions from a heavenly host to go to Bethlehem. The magi arrived in Bethlehem because of their ability to interpret the movement of the stars and planets in the heavens. How can we find that meaningful experience of the good news that "in Christ God was reconciling the world to himself" (2 Cor. 5:19)? Where can we enter imaginatively into the story, feeling the magnitude of God's love and able to consider the challenges and choices that story places before us?

One way that we can relive the story with a feeling of mystery, pageantry, and awe is to feast on the bread and the wine at the Lord's Table. The Eucharist serves as the greatest opportunity we have to relive the birth of Jesus. In this mystery of Holy Communion the love of Christ becomes flesh in us when the celebrant affirms, "May these gifts of bread and wine be for us the body and blood of Christ, that we may be for the world the body of Christ redeemed by his blood" (UMBW 38). In this manner the Word becomes flesh today.

Singing Mary's Song reminds us that God's love for us achieves its goal when we love one another.

1. Where did Jesus, God-With-Us, come to you today?
2. What challenges or barriers—emotional, spiritual, practical—prevented you from experiencing Advent today?
3. What does it mean that God *gave* God's son *for you?*
4. God became flesh over two thousand years ago in the person of Jesus. How can this love be incarnate in you?
5. List the name of one person for whom you will be Christ today, one person to whom God will send you.

Prayer: Loving Creator, you are our God and your name is Love. You love each of us as if there were only one of us to love. Amen.

SATURDAY

In the End a Beginning

SCRIPTURE READING • ROMANS 15:13

Advent brings hope in a fresh start and a confident expectation about what lies ahead. In the story of the great flood (Genesis 6–8), God punished humankind for its sin but saved a remnant: "God remembered Noah and all the wild animals and all the domestic animals that were with him in the ark" (Gen. 8:1). This would result in a new covenant, new direction, and a new world. When the nation of Judah was sent into exile for its sins, God used the opportunity to rebuild the nation and "do a new thing" (Isa. 43:19).

Jürgen Moltmann, a distinguished German theologian, also experienced a new hope that arose from catastrophe. In his book *In the End—The Beginning:*

The Life of Hope, he writes about the destruction of Hamburg, his home city, in July 1943, when Moltmann was seventeen years old. He describes graphically how, night after night, Royal Air Force bombers dropped incendiary bombs, creating a firestorm that killed over forty thousand people and reducing most of the city to rubble. During one of these nighttime raids, a bomb blast killed his best friend; Moltmann, who was standing next to him, was blasted into the water. He awoke holding on to a piece of driftwood, which saved his life. "On that catastrophic night, for the first time in my life," he wrote, "I cried out to God: 'God, where are you?' That was my question in the face of death."

Moltmann was confined for the next two years in a Scottish prisoner-of-war camp. He spent this time searching for answers, not only fighting loneliness and fear about what would become of him but also agonizing over the question that would haunt him the rest of his life: "Why am I still alive and not dead like the rest?" An army chaplain gave him a Bible to read, which became a life-changing experience. Moltmann read at first with little understanding, but when he reached the Gospel of Mark, he began to understand. "When I came to Jesus' death cry: 'My God, why have you forsaken me?' I was profoundly struck. I knew this was the one who understands me. I began to understand the Christ who was assailed by God and suffered from God, because I felt he understood me. That gave me new courage to live. I saw colors again, heard music again, and felt the courage of renewed vitality."

This moment became a turning point in Moltmann's life. "It was here that I arrived at the Christian faith and decided to study theology. I had no idea what the church was about, but I was looking forward to an assurance that would sustain me in my newly found faith." When he returned to Hamburg in 1948, he began to study theology and has become a prominent Christian theologian. Perhaps not surprisingly, one of his most influential works is titled *The Theology of Hope*. For Moltmann, hope was born of catastrophe.

As I have noted, when Mary appeared at the foot of the cross, she remained silent (John 19:25). We can assume that this silence resulted from her grief and pain, from an inability to grasp who her son was and what was happening to him. Her absence on the morning of the Resurrection at the empty tomb may signal her pain and sorrow. Notice that the women who did come to the tomb early that morning brought spices with them (Mark 16:1; Luke 24:1). They were expecting to find a dead body that they hoped to prepare for burial, not to meet a resurrected Lord. When they ran to tell the disciples (who were hiding behind locked doors) that Jesus was alive, they were met with disbelief (Luke 24:11). Mary was not the only person among this small band of followers who suffered from despair.

But events changed quickly. A fifth and final reference to Mary in the New Testament is found in the Book of Acts. All the followers of Jesus who were with him after his resurrection and ascension came together and devoted themselves continually to prayer for the coming of the Holy Spirit in the upper room in Jerusalem. Among the disciples were certain women, "including Mary the mother of Jesus" (Acts 1:14). On the eve of Pentecost we see Mary for the last time as she prays and waits with the disciples in the upper room for the life-giving Spirit of God. Mary no longer has doubts. Now she knows that the promise given to her on that night in Nazareth some thirty years ago, "and of his kingdom there will be no end" (Luke 1:33), is true.

As Mary sang so eloquently so many years ago:

[The Lord's] mercy is for those who fear him
from generation to generation. . . .
He has brought down the powerful from their thrones,
    and lifted up the lowly;
he has filled the hungry with good things,
    and sent the rich away empty.
He helped his servant Israel,
    in remembrance of his mercy,
according to the promise he made to our ancestors,
    to Abraham and to his descendants forever.
                                    —Luke 1:50, 52-55

Natalie Sleeth wrote, "in our end is our beginning. . . . at the last, a victory. Unrevealed until its season, something God alone can see" (UMH 707). In the midst of present-day injustice and violence, which we know so well, God cares, God comes, God loves and redeems. God did that in Moses' day in Egypt. God did that in Jesus' day in Judea. God continues to do that through the Holy Spirit in our day. The angel's last words to Mary were, "For nothing will be impossible with God" (Luke 1:37).

Singing Mary's Song reminds us that the Mighty One has done great things for us; holy is God's name!

1. Where did Jesus, God-With-Us, come to you today?
2. What challenges or barriers—emotional, spiritual, practical—prevented you from experiencing Advent today?

Prayer: God of new beginnings, as we are about to begin our journey through a new year may we remember:

In your will is our peace.
In your love is our rest.
In your service is our joy. Amen.

WRITING YOUR MAGNIFICAT

During Advent, take time to write your own Magnificat. This week write the last verse. Use these questions to guide your work.

- What aid has God offered you?
- What promises have been fulfilled?

LEADER'S GUIDE

SESSION 1: SINGING MARY'S SONG

Participants need to have books in hand at least one week in advance of the first meeting or the first Sunday of Advent. They will begin reading the Sunday prior to the first Sunday in Advent.

PREPARING FOR SESSION 1

- Read the daily readings for Week 1.
- Prepare materials for the worship center (a picture, icon, or image of Mary; an Advent wreath, matches).
- Depending on which option you choose for the "Opening," have one copy of the Magnificat for yourself and a copy for every member to read (collect these for reuse); if you decide to use a musical setting, decide who will lead it and provide hymnals for everyone. (Note that copyrighted material should not be reproduced without written permission from the publisher.)
- Select the discussion questions for "Sharing Responses" and write them on poster board, newsprint, or note cards for display or to pass out.
- Read through the "Exploring the Word" activity until you feel comfortable leading it. Collect the various images of Mary to display.

SET UP

Place a picture, icon, or painting of Mary, along with the Advent wreath, at the center of your gathering space. You may use the same image each week or choose a new one for each session. (Note: All meeting outlines are for forty-five-minute sessions.)

OPENING (5 MINUTES)

- Welcome each person to the group and allow time for introductions.
- Explain to the group that the image at the center of your gathering space is a reminder of the focus on Mary, *Theotokos* (Christ Bearer). She will be our focus of study and reflections for the coming weeks.
- Light the first candle of the Advent wreath and say,

   This week we celebrate that God uses unlikely vessels to bring the message of hope and peace.

- Read the Magnificat, either in unison or aloud to the group, or use a musical setting.
- Then pray this prayer (or one of your choosing):

   Lord, open our hearts to glorify you. Speak to the depths of our souls that we might rejoice in you, our Savior. Amen.

SHARING RESPONSES (15 MINUTES)

- Invite participants to sit in groups of two or three persons. Give the groups a couple minutes to review their responses to the week's scripture experiences.
- Choose from the following list several questions (feeling free to add questions of your own) for use in the smaller groups when discussing each week's Bible reading and responses. You might choose only two or three of the questions for this week's discussion. Pass out the note cards with the questions or hang the poster or newsprint in a visible place.
- Encourage group members to listen for God in each person's words. Remind everyone to allow each group member time to respond to a question before the group moves on to the next.

- What scripture passage from the past week do you remember as especially meaningful? Why?
- How did the daily readings connect to the events in your life this week? Which one was especially appropriate? In what way?
- How did the daily readings encourage you to change some aspect of your behavior?
- What do you want to remember from this week's readings? Why?

• If time allows, invite members to share their insights concerning scripture with the entire group.

EXPLORING THE WORD (20 MINUTES)

Before the meeting, gather as many pictures of Mary—paintings from around your church, icons, downloads from the Internet, Sunday school curriculum—as you can. Try to have at least one picture for each participant.

Option 1

• Place all these pictures face up in the center of the group. Invite each person to spend some time in quiet prayer reflecting on what he or she knows, believes, or imagines when thinking about Mary. When all members are ready, ask them to choose the image that best depicts their concept or understanding of Mary.

• When everyone has chosen an image, have them reform the small groups and share with one another about their mental image of Mary. How much thought has he or she given to the mother of Jesus? How does this image capture that? Allow time for participants to pray for one another, asking God to reveal new insights this Advent through the life and person of Mary.

Option 2

• Place all the pictures in the center of the gathering space face down. Invite each person to select one image randomly. Once everyone has chosen an image, ask participants to meditate on his or her picture using these questions:

- What kind of woman is Mary?
- What is her role?

      – How does she feel?

      – What might she say to you?

- Allow a time for silent reflection, then invite each person to say a few words about the image they chose and to share how he or she responded to the questions.

CLOSING (5 MINUTES)

- Remind the group to read and pray each day, to reflect on the daily questions, and to make notes about insights and questions.
- Sing "Good Christian Friends, Rejoice" (UMH 224) or an appropriate hymn of your choosing.
- Ask for prayer concerns. Then pray this prayer or one of your choosing, mentioning the group's concerns at the end:

> **Lord, with all our hearts we do glorify you. From the depths of who we are, we rejoice in you, our Savior. We ask for your love to work in us and in our world, especially on behalf of _____ [mention concerns named]. Let us be open to what Mary may teach us this Advent. Amen.**

- Extinguish the candle and dismiss the group with these words:

> **Go into the world with eyes to see and voices to sing.**

SESSION 2: IN THE FULLNESS OF TIME

PREPARING FOR SESSION 2

- Read the daily readings.
- Prepare materials for the worship center (a picture, icon, or image of Mary; an Advent wreath, matches).
- Select the discussion questions for "Sharing Responses" and write them on poster board, newsprint, or note cards for display or to pass out.

- Read the "Exploring the Word" activity until you feel comfortable leading it. Make sure you have newsprint and markers.

SET UP

Place a picture, icon, or painting of Mary, along with the Advent wreath, at the center of your gathering space when the group arrives. You may use the same image each week or choose a new one for each session.

OPENING (5 MINUTES)

- Welcome each person to the group this second week of Advent.
- Point out again to the group that the image at the center of your gathering space is a reminder of the focus on Mary, *Theotokos* (Christ Bearer).
- Light the first and second candles of the Advent wreath and say,

  This week we celebrate the fact that God appointed a time and place for Jesus' birth.

- Read (in unison or by yourself) or sing the Magnificat.
- Pray this prayer (or one of your choosing):

  Lord, look down on us now with favor. Open our eyes to the great things you have done for us. Holy is your name. Amen.

SHARING RESPONSES (15 MINUTES)

- Invite group members to sit in groups of two or three persons. Give them a couple minutes to review their responses to the week's scripture experiences.
- Choose from this list several questions (feeling free to add questions of your choosing) for the smaller groups to use when discussing each week's Bible readings and responses. You might choose only two or three of the questions for this week's discussion. Pass out the note cards with the questions or hang the poster or newsprint in a visible place.
- Encourage group members to listen for God in each person's words. Remind everyone to allow each group member time to respond to a question before the group moves on to the next.

- What scripture passage from the past week do you remember as especially meaningful? Why?
- How did the daily readings connect to what has been going on in your life this week? Which one seemed especially appropriate? In what way?
- How did the daily readings encourage you to change some aspect of your behavior?
- What do you want to remember from this week's readings? Why?

• If time allows, invite members to share their insights with the group.

EXPLORING THE WORD (20 MINUTES)

• Tell the group that the lesson today is based on the work of Frank Lake (1914–1982), a psychiatrist in the United Kingdom who developed an insightful way to understand individuals' efforts to find significance and meaning in their lives. He called it the cycle of grace.

• Write the four terms *Acceptance, Achievement, Sustaining Strength,* and *Significance* on the newsprint (without the arrows).

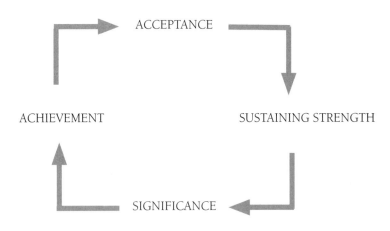

ACCEPTANCE

ACHIEVEMENT   SUSTAINING STRENGTH

SIGNIFICANCE

Acceptance (what Methodists call prevenient grace) is the grace that God extends before a person ever makes a decision to accept God. God accepts people in their sin, before they choose God. God's acceptance is both radical and free.

The realization of and belief in God's acceptance give people *sustaining strength* necessary to make decisions that are healthy, faithful, and obedient. Imagine Jesus, having just been called "beloved" by God at his baptism, able to withstand the temptations in the wilderness.

Those who believe in God's unconditional acceptance and experience this sustaining strength know that they are persons of *significance* and are poised to *achieve* great things. This statement does not grow from pride or arrogance but from the utmost humility, because one's worth is tied to the Creator, the one who calls each of us "Beloved."

- Next, draw the arrows as indicated on the diagram above. Explain that many people try to work this cycle in reverse. Rather than first accepting God's grace, they strive first to achieve great things hoping that their achievements will make them significant in the eyes of others. Rather than embracing God's acceptance and gaining the sustaining strength to be people of significance and achievement, people work hard to *prove* their strength and *earn* their acceptance.

- Invite the members of the group to discuss together how Mary lived this cycle. Mary must have believed in the love of God, accepted the grace offered to her, and demonstrated amazing strength. In that moment, she knew her life to be one of significance and from that moment she "was blessed above all women" (Luke 1:42).

- Allow participants enough time to write down their thoughts or to talk with a partner about how he or she sees the cycle of grace at work in his or her life.

- Close by praying, **Gracious God, in this season of Advent give us pause. Let us slow our lives enough to enter in the cycle of grace—to believe in your acceptance, feel your strength, know our significance and achieve great things for you. Amen.**

CLOSING (5 MINUTES)

- Remind the group to read and pray each day, to reflect on the daily questions, and to make notes about insights and questions.
- Sing "Good Christian Friends, Rejoice" (UMH 224) or an appropriate hymn of your choosing.
- Ask for prayer concerns. Then pray this prayer or one of your choosing, mentioning the group's concerns at the end:

> **Gracious God, we give thanks for your presence with us. We proclaim your favor and worship your holy name. We ask for your love to work in us and in our world, especially on behalf of _____ [mention concerns named]. Amen.**

- Extinguish the candles and dismiss the group with these words:

> **Go into the world confident in God's acceptance and with voices to sing.**

SESSION 3: COMING OUT OF EGYPT

PREPARING FOR SESSION 3

- Read the daily readings.
- Prepare materials for the worship center (a picture, icon, or image of Mary; an Advent wreath, matches).
- Select the questions for discussion in "Sharing Responses" and write them on poster board, newsprint, or note cards so they can be displayed or passed out.
- Read the "Exploring the Word" activity until you feel comfortable leading it. Make sure you have newsprint and markers for yourself and enough paper and pens for each participant.

SET UP

Place a picture, icon, or painting of Mary, along with the Advent wreath, at the center of your gathering space before the group arrives. You may use the same image each week or choose a new one for each session.

OPENING (5 MINUTES)

- Welcome each person to the group this third week of Advent.
- Point out again to the group that the image at the center of your gathering space is a reminder of the focus on Mary, *Theotokos* (Christ Bearer).
- Light the first, second, and third candles of the Advent wreath and say,

  This week we celebrate that, through Jesus, God offers freedom to all.

- Read (in unison or by yourself) or sing the Magnificat.
- Pray this prayer (or one of your choosing):

  We come seeking your mercy, O God. We come in need of your strength. Forgive our arrogance and lift us up. Amen.

SHARING RESPONSES (15 MINUTES)

- Invite group members to sit in groups of two or three persons. Give them a couple minutes to review their responses to the week's scripture experiences.
- Choose from the following list several questions (feeling free to add questions of your choosing) for the smaller groups to use when discussing each week's Bible reading and responses. You might choose only two or three of the questions for this week's discussion. Pass out the note cards with the questions or hang the poster or newsprint in a visible place.
- Encourage group members to listen for God in each person's words. Remind everyone to allow each group member time to respond to a question before the group moves on to the next.
  - What scripture passage from the past week do you remember as especially meaningful? Why?

- How did the daily readings connect to what has been going on in your life this week? Which one was especially appropriate? In what way?
- How did the daily readings encourage you to change some aspect of your behavior?
- What do you want to remember from this week's readings? Why?

• If time allows, invite members to share insights with the entire group.

EXPLORING THE WORD (20 MINUTES)

• Pass out paper and pens. Ask participants to draw a line down the middle of the page, labeling the left-hand column "Season of Advent" and the right-hand column "Season of Christmas." Create the same columns on the newsprint.

• Give everyone three to five minutes to write down words in both columns that describe the feelings, expectations, and tasks that describe both seasons. When the time is up, go around the circle several times, asking each member to share one word from his or her list, and write the words on the newsprint.

• Say to the group: "This week we read about the holy family's journey to Egypt. Our book emphasized that Joseph and Mary were not merely fleeing but also withdrawing. Their time in Egypt was a chance for this young family to reflect on what had happened, to draw close to one another and to God, and to prepare to reenter Israel when the time was right. The writer makes the point that when people travel into the wilderness, "withdrawal is not an end in itself; withdrawal happens for the purpose of return" (page 64).

• Our secular experience of Christmas—all those feelings and experiences on the right-hand side of the newsprint—is the life we need to withdraw from at times. Advent—and all we hope for in the left-hand column—is the withdrawal. Now is the time to prepare, to gain new perspective, and to gain strength for reentry.

• Form small groups of two or three, and discuss how Advent can prepare us to act or react to Christmas in new ways. How might Advent prepare

us for encountering the new year in new and creative ways? You may
want to offer specific scenarios to consider; such as, a busy schedule of
commitments and parties, time for family, the ways we spend money.

- Allow time for each group to share a brief summary or insights from
their conversations.

CLOSING (5 MINUTES)

- Remind the group to read and pray each day, to reflect on the daily
questions, and to make notes about insights and questions.
- Sing "Good Christian Friends, Rejoice" (UMH 224) or an appropriate
hymn of your choosing.
- Ask for prayer concerns. Then pray this prayer or one of your choosing,
mentioning the group's concerns at the end:

> **Gracious God, because of your mercy we go from here
> to show mercy. With our strength renewed we go from
> here to serve and lift up the lowly. We ask for your love
> to work in us and in our world, especially on behalf of
> _____ (mention concerns named).
> Amen.**

- Extinguish the candles and dismiss the group with these words:

> **Go into the world slowly and intentionally, with voices singing.**

SESSION 4: PREPARING FOR JESUS' BIRTH

PREPARING FOR SESSION 4

- Read the daily readings.
- Prepare materials for the worship center.
- Select the questions for discussion in "Sharing Responses" and write
them on poster board, newsprint, or note cards so they can be displayed
or passed out.

- Read the "Exploring the Word" activity until you feel comfortable leading it. You will need newsprint, pens, magazines, newspapers, markers, scissors, and glue.

SET UP

Place a picture, icon, or painting of Mary, along with the Advent wreath, at the center of your gathering space when the group arrives. You may use the same image each week or choose a new one for each session.

OPENING (5 MINUTES)

- Welcome each person to the group this fourth week of Advent.
- Point out again to the group that the central image of your gathering space is a reminder of the focus on Mary, *Theotokos* (Christ Bearer).
- Light all four candles of the Advent wreath and say,

  This week we prepare our hearts for Christ's birth with wonder and expectation.

- Read (in unison or by yourself) or sing the Magnificat.
- Pray this prayer (or one of your choosing):

  O God, we come hungry and in need of aid. We come to hear your promises. Amen.

SHARING RESPONSES (15 MINUTES)

- Invite group members to sit in groups of two or three persons. Give them a couple minutes to review their responses to the week's scripture experiences.
- Choose from the following list several questions (feeling free to add questions of your choosing) for the smaller groups to use when discussing each week's Bible reading and responses. You might choose only two or three questions for this week's discussion. Pass out the note cards with the questions or hang the poster or newsprint in a visible place.
- Encourage group members to listen for God in each person's words.

Remind everyone to allow each group member time to respond to a question before the group moves on to the next.

- What scripture passage from the past week do you remember as especially meaningful? Why?
- How did the daily readings connect to what has been going on in your life this week? Which one was especially appropriate? In what way?
- How did the daily readings encourage you to change some aspect of your behavior?
- What do you want to remember from this week's readings? Why?

• If time allows, invite members to share insights with the entire group.

EXPLORING THE WORD (20 MINUTES)

• Begin by asking group members to name their favorite Christmas songs (secular as well as religious). Write the titles on the newsprint. You may even take time to sing a verse of several of the most popular songs.

• Pass out the copies of the Magnificat (if you haven't already) and tell the group that this represents the first Christmas hymn, the original song of preparation for the coming of Christ. Over the centuries the lyrics may have changed but the message of hope and deliverance often remains in our hymns. In other cases, the songs may seem to celebrate a holiday absolutely foreign to this original hymn.

• Read aloud the following passage (page 94):

> **In the midst of present-day injustice and violence, which we know so well, God cares, God comes, God loves and redeems. God did that in Moses' day in Egypt. God did that in Jesus' day in Judea. God continues to do that through the Holy Spirit in our day. The angel's last words to Mary were, "For nothing will be impossible with God" (Luke 1:37).**

• Then state, **This is our chance to imagine how we participate in the work that God continues this day, correcting, redeeming, and bringing hope and deliverance.**

- Place the newspapers, magazines, markers, scissors, and glue in a central location. Tell each person to use his or her copy of the Magnificat to "rewrite" the words that Mary sang for today. They can write words or phrases from ancient or contemporary hymns; or illustrate the "arrogant" and the "powerful"; and show examples of "aid," "mercy," and "promises" with pictures or headlines. Some may want to rewrite the hymn entirely in their own words.
- When participants are finished rewriting and reinterpreting the Magnificat for their lives today, invite them to share their hymns of hope and deliverance.

CLOSING (5 MINUTES)

- Thank the group members for their faithfulness to the study and for participating. Invite the members to name specific ways that the group has been a blessing for them.
- Sing "Good Christian Friends, Rejoice" (UMH 224) or an appropriate hymn of your choosing.
- Ask for prayer concerns. Then pray this prayer or one of your choosing, mentioning the group's concerns at the end:

Lord, we will fill the hungry. We will offer aid to the empty-handed. And we will participate in your work wherever we can. We ask for your love to work in us and in our world, especially on behalf of _____ [mention concerns named]. Amen.

- Extinguish the candles and send the group forth with these words:

Go into the world singing words of hope and deliverance.

NOTES

Introduction

1. Bonnie Miller-McLemore, *The Blessed One*, ed. Beverly Gaventa and Cynthia Rigby (Louisville: Westminster John Knox Press, 2002), 111.

2. Ibid., 105.

3. John Buchanan, "Hail Mary," *Christian Century* (Dec. 14, 2004): 3.

Week One

1. Viktor E. Frankl, *Man's Search for Meaning* (Boston: Beacon Press, 2006), 40.

2. See Stephen R. Covey, *The Seven Habits of Highly Effective People: Restoring the Character Ethic* (New York: Fireside, 1989): 32–33.

3. Martin Copenhaver, *Journal for Preaching* (Advent, 2007): 35.

Week Two

1. George Arthur Buttrick, *Christ and Man's Dilemma* (Nashville, TN: Abingdon Press, 1956), 122.

2. William Barclay, "Gospel of Luke," *Daily Study Bible* (Philadelphia: Westminster Press, 1956),

3. John R. Claypool, *The Hopeful Heart* (Harrisburg, PA: Morehouse Publishing, 2003), 35ff.

4. Bhatia Pooja, "Haiti's Angry God," *New York Times* (January 14, 2010): A37.

5. Philip Yancey, *What's so Amazing about Grace?* (Grand Rapids, MI: Zondervan, 1997), 281f.

Week Three

1. R. Alan Culpepper, "Gospel of Luke: Introduction, Commentary, and Reflections," in *The New Interpreter's Bible,* volume IX (Nashville, TN: Abingdon Press, 1995), 78.

2. Walter Brueggemann, *The Threat of Life: Sermons on Pain, Power, and Weakness* (Minneapolis: Augsburg Fortress, 1996), 68.

3. N. T. Wright, *Surprised by Hope: Rethinking Heaven, the Resurrection, and the Mission of the Church* (New York: Harper One, 2008), 274.

4. Walter Wink, *Engaging the Powers: Discernment and Resistance in a World of Domination* (Minneapolis: Fortress Press, 1992), 142–3.

Week 4

1. Dag Hammarskjöld, *Markings* (New York: Alfred A. Knopf, Inc., 1966), 51.

2. *Merriam-Webster's Collegiate Dictionary*, 11th ed., s.v. "Ponder."

3. William Barclay, *The Gospel of John* (Philadelphia: Westminster Press, 1956), 1:128.

4. David Rensberger, "God Is Love," *Weavings: A Journal of the Christian Spiritual Life*, XIII no. 1 (1998): 16–22. See also Rensberger's commentary on 1, 2, 3 John in the Abingdon New Testament Commentaries.

5. Jürgen Moltmann, *In the End—The Beginning: The Life of Hope* (Minneapolis: Fortress Press, 2004), 44–46.

•